# Trying Neighbours

# Trying Neighbours

*Some of the trials and misdeeds of Huntingdonshire folk, 1712–1889*

Marion Palmann

The Choir Press

First published in the United Kingdom in 2020 by
The Choir Press

ISBN 978-1-78963-121-0

# Contents

# Preface

This collection came about following the theft of the lead from the roof of All Saints Church in Brington, near Huntingdon, in December 2019. A small band of enthusiasts, committed to keeping this medieval parish church wind and water-tight, had just participated in the re-ordering of the building to provide a fresh, bright community space available for everyone in the village to use. The work had been completed in the September. It was therefore disappointing and frustrating to discover that, in the dead of night on 8 December, someone had peeled off the roof, leaving the ancient timbers blinking at the moon quite possibly for the first time in four or five hundred years. Rain came in overnight, and spoilt the freshly painted interior.

Heroic villagers came to the rescue immediately, to cover the roof with a temporary membrane until the help of the experts could be obtained. In fact, they did this twice in two days, because the church had unwisely picked a week of gales in which to be robbed, and the first coverings did not withstand the onslaught. We could not thank them enough for their generosity and considerable physical exertions.

I wondered how long thieves had been interested in stealing lead from churches, and out of curiosity took a look at old newspaper records. These showed that stealing lead is as old as the hills. It was suggested by the current chair of the parish council that a suitable method of trying lead thieves would be to see if the thief could swim up the river with all his booty tied to his legs: if he could, he would be free to keep it, and welcome.

It occurred to me that one way to make crime pay would be to create a short compendium of some of the criminal trials that had taken place in Huntingdonshire over the last two hundred years or so, and to direct all the proceeds towards the roof repair fund. Also, simply because I have been collecting them over the last twenty or so years, I have included some old images of the villages involved in the cases discussed, which I hope will be of general interest.

This, therefore, is the sole purpose of this collection, and so thank you for helping us to raise funds by purchasing a copy. At the time of going to press, the very small congregation has raised nearly £1000 of the estimated £15,000 that will be needed – including a very kind donation from Choir Press, who have printed this book. If you would like to support us further, you can currently find our campaign on Just Giving, by searching for 'AllSaintsBrington', and we will be very grateful indeed for your support – thank you!

Marion Palmann

1 *Huntingdon Town Hall and Assizes*

# Introduction

Prior to the reorganisation of the English court system in 1971, the miscreants of Huntingdonshire were tried, convicted and punished locally by a three-tier judicial system that had existed for centuries. Both hanging and incarceration were conveniently available in the county town of Huntingdon until well into the nineteenth century.

Minor infractions of the law were dealt with by local justices of the peace; more serious crimes were referred to the quarter sessions, and the most serious cases found themselves in the Huntingdon assizes.

As today, the local justices of the peace were not legally qualified. In the nineteenth century, they were generally selected from amongst local gentry, clergy and landowners. They dealt with minor misbehaviour and breaches of local by-laws, and tried cases without a jury. They also had the power to refer cases to the assizes if they considered them sufficiently serious.

The quarter sessions were (as the name implies) court sittings that were held four time a year, at Epiphany (January), Easter, midsummer and Michaelmas (Autumn). The court consisted of senior justices of the peace. These justices were supported by a legally-qualified (and usually rather well-paid) 'clerk of the peace', and a jury of twelve locally-appointed men. The kinds of cases tried by these quarterly courts were those too serious for the local magistracy, but did not include 'capital'[1] offences, which had to be passed up to the assizes for trial.

The assizes tried criminals on indictment (including for murder, burglary, forgery and other crimes potentially punishable by the death sentence), and also heard civil cases such as contract disputes and land disputes.

Huntingdonshire was part of the ancient Norfolk assize circuit, to which also belonged the counties of Buckinghamshire, Bedfordshire, Cambridgeshire Suffolk and Norfolk. Sessions were held twice a year, at Lent and in the summer, and involved senior judges travelling from one town to another with their retinue of attendants, including personal chaplains.

1. I.e. offences for which the death penalty could be imposed.

The arrival of the judges of the assizes in Huntingdon would literally be greeted with fanfares of trumpets, and was accompanied by processions. On the day of arrival there would be a special church service, at which a senior cleric would be invited to preach the sermon, and there would be a grand dinner – often hosted by the Earl of Sandwich at Hinchingbrooke House. The Sheriff of Huntingdon would have ensured that a suitable grand jury had been picked and was ready to review the cases listed for attention.

The grand jury would be composed of (male) worthies from the county's upper social echelons. Their task was to decide whether there was a 'true bill' against each of the prisoners brought before the court – in other words, whether or not there was a sufficient basis upon which to proceed to a trial. If they found a true bill, the case would be tried, usually immediately, before another jury. If they did not find a true bill, that was the end of the matter, and the prisoner was free to go home.

For those cases that were to go forward to be tried, a 'petty jury' of respectable (male) citizens would have been empanelled. On a finding of guilt, it was not uncommon for the jury to recommended mercy where they had been touched by a sad story.

The sentencing policy is fascinating. There was apparent inconsistency at times, but some trends can be picked out. Throughout the first half of the nineteenth century, a man found to have been violently abusive of (especially female) members of his own family might incur nothing more than a rebuke or a relatively mild punishment. Parental chastisement leading to the death of a child attracted mild criticism. Concealment of the birth of a (usually illegitimate) child would gain the mother significant time in prison. Violation of property, such as burglary, and theft of sheep or horses, often meant the death penalty in the first half of the nineteenth century, although it was often commuted to transportation or lengthy imprisonment. Transportation was common until the second half of the nineteenth century, when it began to be phased out. The last transportation occurred in 1868.

Whereas the magistracy was originally central to the maintenance of law and order (by reading the riot act, and invoking armed assistance when needed), the gradual development of the police force meant that, over time, they lost some of their more administrative civil functions and the role became an increasingly judicial one.

In the 1830s, roughly a quarter of magistrates were clergymen[i]. Whilst appointments were made by the Lord Chancellor, it was generally understood that they would be chosen from amongst names put forward by the borough and town councils. The Lord Chancellor was not short of correspondence on this subject, as there were nearly as many opinions as to how he should exercise his jurisdiction as there were potential candidates. In 1873, a series of reports appeared in the Sheffield press when an unknown citizen (whose identity the Lord Chancellor refused to divulge) had had the temerity to propose two names to his lordship for consideration. His lordship then wrote to the town council to ask them for comments on the two men in question, and the council was by turns astonished and insulted. Whilst there was no legal reason why nominations should be made otherwise than by the council, it just wasn't done. They expended a great deal of energy debating whether to ignore the letter altogether out of sheer pique, or to counter-propose the mayor himself as a candidate, on the grounds that his worship's age and length of service, and the gratitude of the community, made his appointment more appropriate. These were, it seems, the accepted qualifiers for sitting in judgment on the citizenry. In 1874 the Lord Chancellor's post bag took another hit, when Huntingdon's nonconformist community felt it was being deliberately excluded from the magistracy. The Lord Chancellor refused to insert himself into local arrangements, and the result no doubt was that otherwise suitable candidates were overlooked, because their brand of Christianity did not fit.

Until 1906 there were property-owning criteria to be eligible for appointment to the office of justice of the peace, and women were not admitted until 1918.

Vested interests were never far from the surface in both the appointment of magistrates and the discharge of their duties. The case of Gustave Henry Grace (discussed below) heard at the Huntingdon quarter sessions in 1881, demonstrated such prejudice.[ii]

It is worth mentioning here that the sentence of death was quite often passed, but not carried out. We may be quite shocked today to read that a man was condemned to death for stealing a sheep or a horse. As George Savile, 1st Marquis of Halifax put it: 'Men are not hang'd for stealing Horses, but that Horses may not be stolen.' The imposition and subsequent remission of the death penalty seems to have been regarded as a deterrent process: the convict would languish in goal for an unspecified period of time (usually the duration of the assizes) before learning that his death sentence had been commuted to something less final. In the meantime, of course, he was left 'hanging' (so to speak) since he would not know whether it would be commuted or not, and would have plenty of time to think about whether stealing the sheep had been worth all the trouble and worry.

Sentences of death for property theft were increasingly commuted in the years up to 1830, with about 55% being commuted by that year. The number of death sentences given out dramatically dropped by the middle of the century, as the country moved away from capital sentencing for all but the most serious of crimes.[iii]

The magistracy welcomed the arrival of a brand-new treadwheel at Huntingdon gaol in 1867. The treadwheel was constructed to accommodate up to eight prisoners at a time, and the intention was that the laborious rotation of the wheel should produce some tangible benefit or profit for the prison authorities. This was commonly (as at Huntingdon) the grinding of corn.

Those prisoners who were to suffer hard labour were put to the wheel for up to eight hours a day but, reassuringly, were monitored by the prison surgeon, who would regularly weigh them and increase their diet if they lost too much weight. In an extreme case, they would be taken off the wheel until their health permitted them to be put back on it.

At each quarter sessions, statistics were produced to the bench of magistrates by the relevant superintendents of the prison, the police and the workhouse, and these were published in the local press. Thus, the number of those incarcerated, their illnesses, the numbers of crimes committed, the number of prisoners punished for bad behaviour, the number of vagrants and the cost per head to maintain the prisoners were all subject to public scrutiny.

What follows is a selection of cases, taken from the reports of crimes and trials in Huntingdon in the eighteenth and nineteenth centuries. Where it has been possible it includes information about the personal histories of those involved. The famous trial of Walter Horsford, the so-called 'St Neots poisoner', has not been included because, whilst the case is fascinating, it is quite well known, and there are already one or two interesting books specifically on the subject.[2]

> Note on pre-decimal currency:
> For those lucky enough not to remember pre-decimal currency, at the time in which the following events occurred there were twelve 'old' pennies to a shilling, and twenty shillings to a pound. A sovereign was the equivalent of a pound, and a guinea was one pound and one shilling.

---

2 For example, see '*The St Neots Poisoning Case*' by Julia Joyce, available on Kindle.

# Crimes and Misdeeds

## John Pridmore, Winwick, July 1837

John Pridmore was the kind of offspring that might make even his own parents pretend to be out when he called – but, unfortunately for his parents, he never actually left home. It was later said that he had been married, but that he had 'sold' his wife. She may have felt she got the better end of the bargain.

In an outpouring of parental pride, untroubled by foresight, he had been named after his father, John Pridmore senior. Mr Pridmore was an agricultural labourer who had been born in Northamptonshire in about 1771, but had come to live and work in Gidding. He married a Gidding girl named Sophia, and they had at least five children. John was their second child (but their eldest son), and was born and baptised in Winwick in 1805.

On Monday, 24 July 1837, after an altercation in the family, John turned both his parents out of their cottage and sent them to spend the night under a haystack.

Two days later, on the $26^{th}$, he returned to the family's cottage after work and demanded his supper. Mrs Pridmore told him that there was the same for him as there had been for his father, namely some tea and some bread. Her son seems to have considered that he was entitled to special treatment, for on hearing this he said he would not be treated in that way, picked up his mother's teapot and threw it out of the door. He then took hold of his mother and turned her out of the house, telling her that she could go back to the haystack, and swore that two out of the three of them would be dead before midnight.

His father then tried to get into bed, which is perhaps a slightly curious thing to do when your wife has just been ejected from your house. John took

2 *Great Gidding, turn of the nineteenth century.*

3 *Shop at Great Gidding.*

hold of his father and pulled him out of it. He dragged him outside and to a nearby horse pond, with the old man calling out 'My dear son! Spare my life this night!' When it became clear that John was not going to relent, he called out 'God have mercy on my soul!' but his son replied 'No! Damn you!' and said he would throw him in head-first so that he would be sure drown more quickly. With that, he grabbed his father by both ankles and tossed him head-first into the water.

Mr Pridmore managed to crawl out of the pond through a briar patch, and then took himself off into the village. It was so late at night that everyone had gone to bed, but he managed to get to the public house, where he stayed the rest of the night, since he was too frightened to go home.

In the reports of the trial, no one addressed the question of what Mr Pridmore thought was happening to poor Sophia, who had been thrown out into the night. He does not appear to have gone to look for her, or to ensure that she was safe.

Meanwhile, having seen the fate of her husband (and displaying rather more matrimonial consideration), Sophia had run to the house of a neighbour, Thomas Gear, and had woken him up, begging him to come and help get her husband out of the water. Mr Gear went off towards the pond, leaving Sophia to take refuge in his house. Unfortunately, her son had followed her there, and he went into the house and attacked her, knocking her to the ground. He dragged her back to her own house and locked her in, saying that he was going to go and check that his father was properly drowned. If not, he said, he would take care of the matter.

As Thomas Gear was making his way to the pond to see if he could help Mr Pridmore, he met John, who threatened him that he, too, would end up in the pond if he didn't leave the old man to drown where he was. Mr Gear replied that, in that case, he would just go back to bed – and so he did. In fact, Mr Gear had actually overheard poor Sophia being dragged away from his house, shouting 'Murder! Murder!' but took no further steps that night to help either Sophia or her husband: he said at the trial that he was just too frightened of their son's reputation for violence.

Sophia managed to break out of the cottage when her son's back was turned, and ran to a cart shed where she hid inside one of the carts. She could hear John searching for her outside, and wrapped her apron round her head so the sound of her breathing would not give her away. She was utterly terrified. For the rest of the night, she just walked around in the dark.

What defence could such a son possibly present to the jury?

His version of events was that he had quarrelled with his father that night, and that they had walked to the horse pond together, and his father had voluntarily climbed into it. Not surprisingly, John was found guilty of attempted murder at the Lent assizes in 1838, and was sentenced to death. His death sentence was later commuted to transportation for life.

4 *Cottages at Winwick Hill, Hamerton Road.*

5 *The windmill, Great Gidding.*

He was kept in the prison hulk *Leviathan* while he waited for his passage. The gaoler's report of his stay on board stated that his character was 'very bad'. He was taken to Van Diemen's Land (now Tasmania) aboard the *Marquis of Hastings* a year later, on 16 March 1839. His crossing took about eighteen weeks.

6 *Prison-ship in Portsmouth Harbour, convicts going aboard.v*

Very little of him can be gleaned in Tasmania, although it is perhaps ironic that he appeared as one of a number of victims of a kidnapping and robbery that took place in 1843. He, with a number of other servants and the family of his master, were taken at gunpoint to the house of a neighbour, trussed up with rope and made to sit on the floor on pain of death, whilst the robbers stole everything they could lay hands on.[iv]

# Disorderly bakers: Brington, April 1867

At this date, there existed a communal oven in Brington, where certain cottagers could take their bread to be baked. Of course, an oven only holds so much: sharing an oven meant there was a need for neighbourly give and take. If they didn't share nicely, there could be trouble.

On 2 April 1867, a baker named Edward Burswell was in charge of the operation of the oven. A woman named Keziah Laxton was baking her loaves, and others were waiting their turn. Keziah's bread had been in the oven for over four hours. She said that the oven was very 'slack' (i.e. cool) and that it was taking a long time to get them baked.

Mr Burswell got fed up with waiting for her. There was a dispute later in court as to which one of them started the pushing and shoving, but the upshot was that Burswell took Keziah's bread out of the oven, and she was shoved onto the ground and dislocated her finger.

Burswell, in his defence, said that Keziah was a woman who liked to tease her neighbours by keeping them out of the use of the oven, and that consequently nobody in Brington was prepared to bake with her. He had asked her civilly to take her bread out, because there were several others waiting to use the oven, and the next day was Sunday, when of course no baking could be done. When she had ignored him, he had removed it for her. As a baker, he said, he knew when bread was cooked and when it wasn't.

The magistrates found him guilty of assaulting her. They fined him four shillings, with the usual 'option' of fourteen days in prison in lieu of payment. Burswell was very clear that he would go to prison rather than pay a penny of the fine.

## Murder of Elizabeth Pare, Great Gidding, January 1716

The following was an eyewitness account of the aftermath of a brutal highway murder that took place between Thurning and Luddington on 9 January 1716, published in the Stamford Gazette:

> *19 Jan. 1716*
>
> *On Wednesday the 9th instant, was committed in Thurning Field one of the most Execrable and Barbarous Murders that ever was heard of, on the body of Mrs Elizabeth Pare, Widow, of Great Gidding in the County of Huntingdon. She received Six or Seven Wounds in her Face and Throat, either of which would (I suppose) have been mortal; her left Hand was so near cut off that it hung only by a Piece Skin, two of her Fingers and one of her thumbs were cut off, and found in the Feld next Morning, together a with large Piece of Flesh cut from one of her Eye-brows; her Legs also were*

*cut so deep that the Marrow in the Bone was discerned. There are some who pretend to exact in numbering her Wounds, that say she had Fifteen, and that Ten of them were mortal; but this you may depend upon, I myself saw Thirteen, and tho' I had been acquainted with her several Years, I knew her mangled Body only by the Apparel that covered it.*

*This horrid Murder was committed about Five a Clock in the Evening, in the Mid-way between Thurning and Luddington, and within Call of both Towns, her Shrieks and Cries were heard by several People of the latter, particularly by a Farmer, who might have assisted her in two Minutes' Time, yet did no more than go into his own House and tell what lamentable Cries he heard. The Consternation the Neighbourhood was in, gave the Murderer Opportunity to escape that Night; but the Day following Henry Johnson of Great Gidding was suspected and examin'd, by some Gentlemen of Thurning, and on Friday the 11th was carried before the Hon. Sir Matthew Dudley, Bart, of Clapton, where upon strict Search, his Shirt and the Right Hand Pocket of his Breeches were found Bloody, which Discovery put the Prisoner into great Surprize, yet he obstinately denied the Murder but after long Examination, he making but trifling Defence, and many strong Circumstances of his Guilt appearing, he was committed to Huntingdon Goal by the said Sir Matthew Dudley.*

*I had like to have forgot to tell you, that the Murder was done with a Hatchet, which is still bloody; and that Mrs Pare was robb'd of about three pound in Money, besides Rings. Thus, Sir, have I sent you a faithful Account of this sad Murder, on the Truth of which you may safely depend. I having related nothing but what I was an eyewitness and ear witness of. I am told that you have already received an account of the Death of the Decease'd, and the proceedings against the Murderer, which if I am not misinform'd, is very different from Truth; I therefore send you this to prevent your being imposed on, and your imposing on others.*[vi]

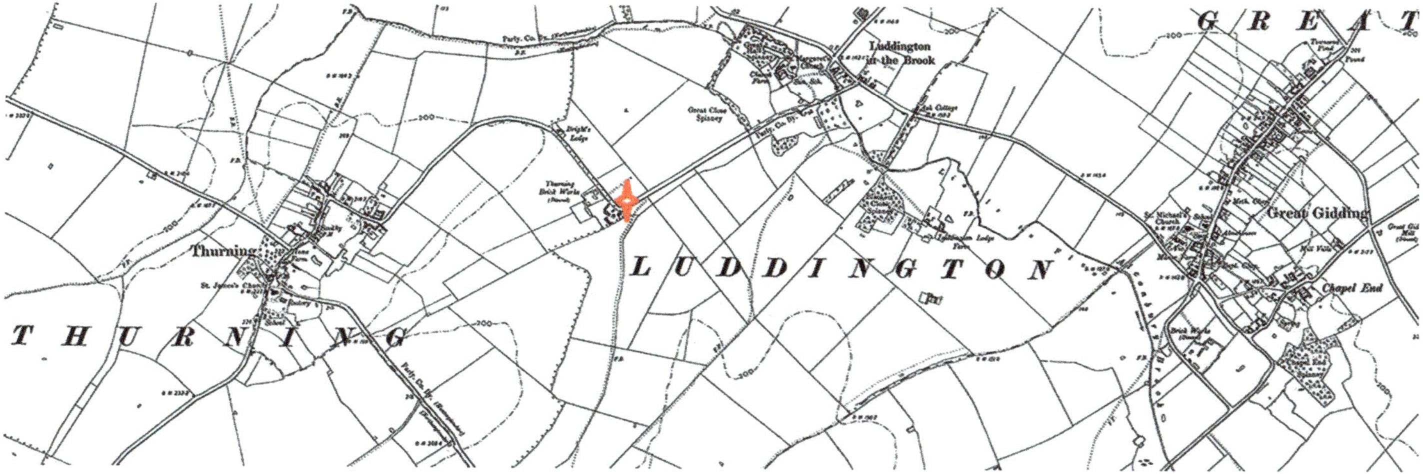


7 *The approximate place of Mrs Elizabeth Pare's demise.*

# Getting away with murder: George Leeton, Stonely, 1868

Sarah Leeton was a widow who lived in Stonely with her eldest surviving son, George. She had been born and raised in Kimbolton. Her husband had come to the village from Warmington near Oundle, and had been a farm labourer, but he had died some ten years before the tragic events of 29 July 1868. The couple had had at least eight children, and all those who lived to adulthood had remained living close by.

George was forty-eight at the date of these events, but seems to have had no home of his own and so was sharing his widowed mother's extremely cramped cottage. His mother was eighty-three.

Although George was in work as a labourer, his mother had no income to live on, and was forced to survive on parish relief. This was not a situation that was acceptable to the parish authorities: that a working man should live in the same house with a parent who was being supported by the parish was regarded as quite shameful. George had been told by the parish relieving officer that unless he ensured that his mother was supported by him, she would have to go into the workhouse. George was quite clear that he had no intention of supporting his mother.

The descriptions of George given in the newspaper reports of subsequent events were not exactly complimentary – his neighbours considered him to be a nuisance and a scrounger. One witness said that George had had a wife, but that he had 'sold' her, which seems to have been a popular activity in Huntingdonshire. He had, in fact, married a young Kimbolton woman named Sophia Robinson in 1854, but they had not remained together long. Sophia appears to have reverted gratefully to her maiden name and to have acquired several children whose paternity remains a mystery to the official record keepers, if not to the community at the time.

This unhappy set of circumstances meant that George had made his home with his mother in Park Lane, Stonely, in a tiny cottage with just one bedroom on the ground floor, which they had to share.

Sarah's neighbour, Mary Barber, used to keep an eye on Sarah, and sometimes take her a cup of tea. Mary had frequently overheard George abusing his mother, but about the middle of July in 1868 an argument had broken out between George and Sarah, in which George was heard to tell his mother that he would 'do for her'.

Mary had last seen Sarah alive on Wednesday 29th July 1868, when Sarah had been relatively fit and well. During that evening, at about half-past ten, two neighbours – Francis Perrett and George Deane – had spotted George in the road and had spoken to him, but George had ignored them. They said that he appeared to be deep in thought, and found his behaviour quite odd.

At about 3.20 the next morning, James Merrill, whose cottage was about fifty yards from Sarah's, was woken by a hammering at his front door, and when he opened it he found George, who asked him to send his wife to Sarah's cottage because his mother was dead. Mrs Merrill was not keen to go with him. She told the court later that she was afraid of George and didn't trust him. He had a nasty reputation for playing tricks on people. Mr Merrill therefore went himself, and discovered Sarah's body lying sideways across her bed, with the bedclothes tossed about, as if she had been in a struggle. The bed quilt was wrapped tightly about her neck and was covering her nose. There was a little blood spattered about, and Sarah's right hand had been deeply slashed. One of her legs was terribly cut and injured, as if it had been pushed onto a metal object, probably the frame of the bed. George's bed didn't seem to have been slept in. They called Sarah's daughter-in-law to come and help attend to the old lady.

Later that morning, George complained bitterly to Mary Barber that his mother had given him a black eye. He told Mary that he and his 83-year-old mother had actually fought, and that he had held her down on her bed until she had gone quiet, and eventually cold. The neighbours all commented that George showed no emotion or grief at his mother's death whatsoever.

Dr Charles Sprague was called to carry out a post-mortem examination later that day. He believed the bruising on Sarah's face had been caused by a fist. He found that her death had actually been the result of suffocation, and had been inflicted with great violence.

Sarah's own village doctor, Dr Ferney, had known her for forty years, and gave evidence that she was never very well, suffering from a persistent cough and being generally very frail. It would not have taken very much force to kill her.

That evening, PC Hammond arrested George on suspicion of killing his mother. His response was 'she hit me first'.

The following day, 1 August, George gave a statement to the police saying that he had gone home to the cottage at about twenty minutes to eleven on the night in question, and had asked his mother what there was for his dinner. She had told him there was cold meat and potatoes, and a piece of cold pudding.

He had made his meal, and then he said that his mother had suddenly attacked him for no reason, so that he had had to manhandle her into her bed. She refused to stay, saying that the room was full of sticks and there were sticks beneath her bed, and in the ensuing tussle she had given him a black eye and had bitten and scratched him. To get her to 'stay put' he had used force to hold her down, and he was aware of her becoming colder and colder until he thought she was dead. That was when he had gone to the Merrills and had asked them to come and attend to her.

At the trial, George could not afford to pay for representation, but the judge used his discretion to provide him with legal counsel. He was represented by Mr Merrewether, a very well-known lawyer on the Huntingdon circuit. As the defendant in the case, George was not permitted to give any evidence on his own behalf. The only evidence given was by the neighbours and the medical experts.

Mr Merrewether had his work cut out to produce any kind of positive impression of George on the jury, and his first effort was to dwell on the fact that none of the neighbours had been able to prove that George habitually abused his mother.

He suggested that the argument, which had resulted in the use of force, could easily have been about Sarah having to go into the union workhouse, and it might have made her frantic, resulting in the need for George to forcibly prevent her from running out of the cottage. This was an interesting conjecture, but not a scenario that George himself had suggested when he was making his statement to the police – and if this is how it had happened, it is unfathomable that he would not have said so in order to exculpate himself. Mr Merrewether said that George's statement was not actually inconsistent with that scenario, even though he had not told the police that was what had occurred.

He also said that the prosecution had not sufficiently proved that George was responsible for Sarah's death; although all the medical evidence had shown that she had been violently suffocated, Dr Ferney had initially equivocated when he was attending the scene, and had been unable at first to determine the cause of death. He had changed his mind by the date of the trial and gave evidence that he believed she had died from suffocation. This evidential 'wobble' gave Mr Merrewether a chance to introduce a note of doubt.

He also said that, whilst George did not deny that he had restrained her, it could have been Sarah's inherent fragility that lead to her death.

Finally, he said that George was in fact a tender-hearted and affectionate son, and suggested that there was no evidence to the contrary.

Readers may be surprised to learn that the jury found George not guilty. Mr Merrewether could congratulate himself on having created enough of a doubt in their minds whether George was the cause of his mother's death, that they did not feel they could hang him for it. They did not even bring in a verdict of manslaughter, which would have been an option if they felt the prosecution had not established enough deliberate intent on his part. Surely George must have been the most surprised of all present when he was discharged without a blemish on his record.

He must have found neighbour relations a bit sticky at the conclusion of his trial: there is nothing quite like living in the midst of a community that believes you murdered your mother and got away with it, to make life awkward. There is no further trace of him in the area after these events.

## The Catworth Riot: December 1885

During the winter months on a farm, when there was less work to be done, some farmers would let men go for the season and then re-hire in the spring. Others would keep their labourers on, but reduce their wages for the winter. In the winter of 1885, it would appear that many local farmers had opted to do the latter, and the men and women affected by the cuts found it unacceptable – no doubt because they found it hard to make ends meet. This particular year wages were reduced by a shilling per week, and it caused some local tempers to boil over.

On the night of 19 December, a group of about sixty men and women from Catworth went on the rampage, doing the rounds of all the farmers who had cut labourers' wages. They noisily demanded that the cuts be restored, otherwise they threatened that they would strike and operate pickets to prevent anyone else working for the farmers concerned.[vii]

They made their way to Tilbrook Grange, the home of Mr Benjamin Measures, by which time feelings were running very high – despite the fact that not a single member of the mob was actually employed by Mr Measures. They surrounded his house, and one of them men knocked on the door. Mr Measures himself was ill in bed, but his wife answered the door and received

8 *Tilbrook Grange, scene of the Catworth Riot (by kind permission of Mr James Hunter).*

the same demands and threats from the crowd outside. She then closed the door on them. Someone in the crowd began to shout that if Mr Measures came out, they would kill him; someone else began throwing stones, and windows were soon broken.

The next morning, Mr Measures went out to survey the damage and found that the mob had torn down several of his fences, and thrown one of them into his pond.

These events in Catworth were reported in almost every town and city in the country, including Scotland, so important was the issue to farmers throughout the nation.

Rather oddly, given the circumstances of a riotous crowd uttering personal threats and invading a person's home, the matter was dealt with not at the assizes, but at the petty sessions before the St Neots magistrates. In fact, it would appear that only one member of the mob could be identified as having committed any offence, and that was Isaac Berridge.

The village constable, PC Middleton, was about his beat on Christmas night and seeing a gaggle of men talking by the cross in the village he strained his ears to hear what they were saying. He overheard Isaac Berridge telling the other men that he had flung the stones at Mr Measures' windows. Berridge was arrested and charged with causing the damage. He appeared in court on 31 December.

In his defence, Berridge asserted that what PC Middleton had actually heard him say was, that he might *just as well* have thrown the stones at the house. The magistrates were not won over by this argument and found him guilty. Mr Measures asked the magistrates not to deal severely with Berridge: he didn't wish to be punitive, he merely wished to ensure that he was protected from such behaviour in the future. Berridge was fined £2 with 18 shillings in costs, and given the option of a month in prison as an alternative.[viii]

9 *Gt. Catworth, corner of High Street and Church Road.*

## The murder of Rev. Joshua Waterhouse: Lt. Stukeley, 1827

Joshua Waterhouse was the rector both of Lt. Stukeley and of Coton, near Cambridge, when his career was brought to an abrupt and violent end in July 1827.

Waterhouse was born in 1746 in Hayfield, Derbyshire, the youngest of four children. His father, a farmer, wished to give Joshua a chance to rise in life through education. He sent him to St Catherine's College, Cambridge (then called 'Catharine's Hall'), where he studied divinity and eventually – but not with much enthusiasm on the part of his colleagues – became a Fellow of the college. As such, he was automatically entitled to the living at (i.e. to become rector of) the parish of Coton, by reason of a custom then some 200 years old. He was not a popular Fellow, and seems to have been in constant fights with his colleagues who, in 1795, raised an unsuccessful petition to try to have him removed.[ix]

When the Master of the college, Dr Lowther Yates, died in 1799, Waterhouse (as Senior Fellow) called the five Fellows together in order that a new Master could be elected from amongst their number. Of the five votes, he attracted two, and the other three were divided between other Fellows. Despite the fact that his majority was insufficient to comply with the rules, he promptly considered himself elected, and moved himself into the Master's Lodge. It must have been quite a humiliation, therefore when he was ordered out a few months later. It is perhaps no wonder that he was deeply unpopular with his colleagues.

If unappealing to his peers, however, the same cannot be said of the female sex: as a young man, Joshua Waterhouse seems to have exhibited great promise as an eligible and popular bachelor. He is said to have been tall, handsome, witty, 'polished', and to have been very much admired by the ladies.

10 *Mary Wollstonecraft by John Williamson 1826–1885.*

Amongst his most surprising conquests was the famous early feminist author, Mary Wollstonecraft, the mother of Mary Shelley.[x]

The exact details of his first encounter with Mary Wollstonecraft are lost to history, but it is known that Waterhouse was a frequent visitor to Bath and Bristol, where he moved in very fashionable circles. This was a place in which Mary Wollstonecraft was known to have resided in around 1787, at which date she and Joshua seem to have entered into a passionate correspondence that continued for some years. The letters were at one time scattered around the kitchen of the rectory, but were lost following his death.

These were not the only love letters that the Reverend Waterhouse received: he seems to have been the object of many a fluttering heart over the years, and is said to have quipped that he had enough love letters to fuel the fire to cook an entire wedding feast if he had been so inclined. But he was not so inclined: he never married, and after his death his two nephews, who went to clear his house, filled an entire sack with these letters and disposed of them.

It was said that as a result of 'early disappointment', or perhaps simply from eccentric habits, Rev. Waterhouse had separated himself from society, and lived the life of a miserly recluse. He lived in the enormous rectory at Little Stukeley with no other company than his dogs, and, not requiring more than a couple of rooms for his personal needs, he turned the remaining rooms over to his 'agricultural hobbies'. Every other room of the house was used for the storage of his grain, fruit and wool crops. He was said to be more attached to his pigs and cows than to any human being, and as a result of not being prepared to pay the 'going rate' for agricultural labour, he had to do most of the work on his farm himself. He used to drive his pigs and cattle to Huntingdon market on foot every Saturday, which was regarded as a most curious thing for a rector to do.

Under his peculiar usage, the rectory fell into alarming disrepair. In order to avoid having to pay the window tax, he blocked up all but two of the rectory

11 *Little Stukeley Rectory as it appeared in 1827.*[xi]

12 *The Swan and Salmon, Little Stukeley.*

windows, making it a dark, airless and forbidding place. It is said that the grain he stored in the house actually sprouted on his carpets, that 'scores of pigs disported before the rectory door' and the gardens were left to grow into a wilderness.

Briefly, he regained some interest in himself and in his home: it was rumoured that he was intending to marry, and he reached into the cobwebs of his wallet to spend about £300 on new furniture, curtains and furnishings for a small portion of the house. He had some of his sacks of corn and sheep fleeces removed to enable some comfortable accommodation to be created. Nobody knew the identity of the prospective bride, but sadly, for reasons we will never know, no wedding ever took place, and the house returned to its former squalor.

He avoided all contact with his parishioners other than the essential attendance at divine service, and if the poor were misguided enough to call at the rectory for alms or assistance, they could expect to be ejected in short order and with a vigour quite surprising for an elderly man. On one occasion he was reported to have spotted what was described as 'a sturdy mendicant' outside the church during a service. As soon as his sermon was over and the clerk was handing out the psalm, he rushed out of the pulpit, threw his surplice off at the church door and roundly laid into the man, literally thrashing him off the premises.

13 *The lovely Parson Trulliber.*[xiii]

As a priest, it is said that Rev. Waterhouse was not respected by his flock, who considered that his personal life had not set the kind of example they were entitled to expect of a clergyman. However, it was notable that often when he read from the gospel or delivered a sermon, the pious words would cause him to burst into tears in front of the congregation. He was a man of many contradictions.

He was known to have strong views about the mode of dress required of his parishioners when attending church, and would refuse to allow anyone wearing a smock to take part in a service. He himself, however, rarely adopted clerical dress, and was almost always to be seen wearing a grubby blue coat, and corduroy trousers. He was not known for his fastidious habits in the personal hygiene department, either: when his clothes got soiled from a day spent close to nature, he used to take himself down to his fishpond and clean himself up without removing his clothes. It was said that he would have made a good model for 'Parson Trulliber' in Henry Fielding's tale of *Parson Andrews.*[xii]

The reverend had had a number of servants over the years, but had found reason to dismiss them all, one by one, until he was left entirely alone in the house. The only recipient of his generosity seems to have been his former housekeeper, Mary Martin, to whom he used to make gifts of money. A daily char woman and a young girl came in to do the domestic work (and occasionally they were also pressed to work in the fields), and he employed a couple of young lads to help with the pigs. He was a churlish master, and the boys were rather afraid of him.

He used to take his breakfast early with the domestics in the kitchen in the morning, and even turned his hand to the cooking; but he would then take himself off to attend to his agricultural pursuits, which were the chief concern of his life. Altogether, including some lands at Coton, he farmed about 150 acres, which were ripe for harvesting in the July when he was helped off with his mortal coil.

Towards the end of his life, he was plagued by break-ins committed by certain of the village boys, and by Joshua Slade in particular. These young thugs used to break in and steal his belongings on a regular basis, but although Waterhouse would get the constable to recover his things from the Slade's cottage, he would never prosecute the culprits for fear (it was said) that his own immoral and unacceptable behaviour would be aired in public.

Slade had been born in Great Stukeley, the third of nine children in a desperately poor family. Education was a luxury they could not afford. He was in trouble a good deal in the village for pilfering as a boy but it, was said, was not without native intelligence: even his mother said of him after his conviction that had he been a scholar, he would have become a forger. Can there be greater praise for a son from his mother?

The family had been turned out of their home in Gt. Stukeley because of debts, and were housed in Little Stukeley at the cost of the parish, upon which they relied for financial support. Joshua had actually been in Rev. Waterhouse's employment on his farm at one point, but at the time of these events was unemployed due to his having been dismissed for stealing from his employer, a local farmer named Stannion.

14 *Joshua Slade, from a drawing made during his trial.*

It was whilst living at Little Stukeley that Slade fell in with an accomplice, William Heddings, said to be an 'incorrigible rascal', and together they seem to have enjoyed an unrestrained spree of burglaries throughout the surrounding villages, but especially at the rectory, which was considered an easy target. It was just such an excursion that was to lead to poor Waterhouse's murder.

Slade's plan had been to break into the rectory while it was light, to hide inside until it was dark, and then to help himself to whatever he could conveniently lay hands on after nightfall and make off with it. The first part of his plan succeeded, in that he gained entry, and stowed himself away in a cupboard in a corridor leading off the kitchen. Unfortunately, having fallen asleep in there, Slade began to snore, and Rev. Waterhouse heard him all too clearly just before 11 o'clock in the morning. No man who was capable of thrashing a 'sturdy mendicant' on church premises was going to shrink from setting about an audacious young burglar in his cupboard, and so he did.

Unfortunately, Slade was armed with a sword, which it later transpired he had stolen from the Horse & Jockey (later called The Waterloo) public house in Huntingdon. He had seemingly taken this item with him as a means of self-protection, and he now found he needed it – but what he did with it was to cut poor Rev. Waterhouse's throat.

Waterhouse fell back into a large trough used for brewing beer, and there he lay, not yet dead, but dying.

Outside, a number of people had heard his screams, and had noticed the dogs barking madly in the yard, but so used were they to aberrant behaviour on the part of the rector that no one bothered to investigate.

A little while later the two young pig attendants, William Parker, aged fourteen (and described as 'a dull looking boy'[xiv]), and Reuben Briggs, aged eleven, came into the house for their lunch, and heard the most terrible groans emanating from the corridor. They could see Rev. Waterhouse lying in the tub with his legs dangling over the side. They had been on the receiving end of many teasing tricks by their employer in the past, and were afraid this was another one. Consequently, they didn't stop to investigate the noises, but ran out of the house and across the road to a neighbour and told her what they had heard. She, likewise, said she thought it was another of the reverend's tricks, and that he was probably drunk. She allowed them to remain in her house to finish their meal. It was later said that had assistance been given to him at this point, he might have been saved.

A little later, two other neighbours, Frederick Rogers and William Ashby, called at the rectory and, receiving no answer to their knocking on the door, went into the house and found the poor man in the tub – but too late, as he was, by now, quite dead. He had sustained a number of wounds, but the principal blow across the jaw and to the throat appeared to be the cause of his death.

An inquest was held at The Bell public house in Lt. Stukeley later the same day, and it became apparent that the chief suspect was Joshua Slade. He contended that he had spent the previous evening drinking in various public houses in Huntingdon and Godmanchester, and had spent the night at his sister's house. She cheerfully corroborated his story. Slade was taken by a police constable to the public houses he had named, in order to check the truth of his statements, and was found to have made the story up. The finger of suspicion now pointed firmly in his direction.

Blood stains were discovered on his clothing, and in an impressive early example of sleuthing, the police managed to confirm that footprints outside the rectory matched Slade's hobnail boots. It was revealed that another of Slade's sisters had also been in Rev. Waterhouse's employment until about two weeks before the murder, but had been dismissed by him because he believed her to have been complicit in an earlier burglary, when 'someone' had secreted himself in the house until nightfall in order to steal his watch and some money. After the dismissal of his sister, Slade was heard to say that he would like to kill the old man.

An investigating officer was sent from Bow Street. The Slade family's cottage was searched and was found to be crammed with stolen goods. The whole family – mother, father and two sons – were charged with crimes related to burglaries in Alconbury, Stow Longa, Broughton and Wood Walton. Joshua Slade was charged with the murder of Mr Waterhouse. The Rev. Dr Maltby (of whom we shall hear more in another tale) was one of the magistrates at his committal.

At first, Slade steadfastly denied that he had killed Mr Waterhouse. He exhibited no emotion in court when the details of the murder were read out before the grand jury, who were to decide whether or not there was a 'true bill'.

The grand jury had no trouble at all in finding that there was a true bill, and Slade went straight on to a trial for murder.

At the trial, Slade's good friend, Heddings, was brought from Huntingdon gaol where he was awaiting trial for other offences, and gave evidence that Slade had admitted his guilt to him, saying that he had been forced to do it when the old man had come at him angrily when he had discovered him hiding in the cupboard. Slade's cool response to this damning evidence was to say that he and Heddings had talked together about who might have committed the murder, but had decided that another (named) man in the village must have done it, and that Heddings had said he was sorry the old man was dead, because he had been hoping to steal a quarter of barley from him the following week.

The judge, in his summing-up, told the jury that there was a mass of circumstantial evidence and that no English jury could rely upon it to deprive the prisoner of his life without other evidence specifically linking him to the crime. That evidence came only from Heddings, who was a convicted felon against whom a death sentence had once been given (although remitted), and who had a history of gaol-breaking. Having heard this guidance, this particular English jury promptly found Slade guilty.

The judge will no doubt have felt less cut-up about the verdict when he later learned that Slade gave a full confession of his guilt before he was hanged. The confession occasioned a stay of execution whilst an investigation was carried out into the other parties (including Heddings) that he implicated in the murder. Slade told them where he had thrown the sword, and they were able to retrieve it from bushes not far from the rectory.

He seems to have undergone a complete change in his attitude, from staunch denial to abject penitence, in the days leading up to his execution. It was said that he paid great attention to the prison chaplain and to prayer, although he never once cried. He said that this was not because of a lack of emotion, but because in all his life he had never been able to do so, though he thought it might much relieve him if he could. He expressed himself grateful for enough days before the sentence was carried out to enable him to make his peace with God.

Finally, the day came, and Slade was shackled and taken on a cart from the old gaol (situated in Orchard Lane in Huntingdon) and transported to the gallows on Mill Common. More than 4000 people had gathered to witness the execution. Slade made a short speech demonstrating his complete repentance for the crime, and then the execution was carried out. The date was 1 September 1827.

It was not quite the end of Joshua Slade, however, for he yet had a significant service to render to his country: the least an executed felon could do was to allow the surgeons to profit by dissecting his body in the interests of medical science. He had no choice in the matter, of course.

Slade was dissected in front of a crowd of fascinated surgeons and medical students. It would be prurient to dwell on the matters they found of interest, as they all seemed to point to a miserable and deprived existence, entirely consistent with his unfortunate upbringing. It was said that 'his countenance seemed a fitting index to the mind of a murderer – cruel, deliberate, and ferocious.' A death mask was made, and one must wonder why, and where that item is today. It was reported in the Glasgow Herald that before his death, knowing that he was to be dissected, he extracted a promise that what was left of him would be buried in his native parish of Stukeley. There is nothing to tell us whether that is what occurred, but the norm was burial within the gaol precincts.[xv]

His family did him no credit. It was reported that:

> *in persons of their condition it would be absurd to expect the acuteness of feeling and nice sensibility which shed an indescribable charm over the intercourse of intelligent and refined society; but the Slades appear to be wanting even in the common humanity. His sisters were not ashamed to attend the races, whilst their brother was immured in a solitary cell, under sentence of death. The mother talks of Joshua's guilt, and of his vicious habits, without the least display of parental feeling.*[xvi]

On the night before the hanging, his father had called at the prison to see if his son had left him anything – old clothes or medicine bottles, or anything that he might be able to sell. It is perhaps hardly Joshua's fault that he grew up without developing the empathy that is essential to acquiring a conscience.

It is very sad to say that even after Rev. Waterhouse's death, the rectory was further burgled and more of his possessions were stolen.

Rev. Waterhouse was buried at Lt. Stukeley, where his tomb can still be seen today, with its brief description of the awful event that terminated his life. It bears the following curious verse:

*Beneath this tomb his mangled body's laid*
*Cut, stabbed and murdered by Joshua Slade;*
*His ghastly wounds a horrid sight to see*
*And hurled at once into Eternity.*
*What faults you've seen in him take care to shun*
*And look at home –*
*Enough's there to be done!*
*Death does not always warning give,*
*Therefore be careful how you live.*

Many years later, in about 1870, a book that was formerly the property of the famous actor, Edmund Kean, was discovered with Rev. Waterhouse's epitaph copied out onto the fly leaf, and beneath it, Kean (who clearly took exception to the verse's rustic, rather than literary, qualities) had added a further verse of his own:

*Worse than Slade, thou murderer of verse*
*Deserving more than he the culprit's hearse!*
*Slade killed the living, perhaps by hunger led*
*You, by your doggerel, have damned the dead!*[xvii]

## The starvation of Martha Crewe: Stilton, 1856

The story of Martha Crewe is a heart-rending one. The kind of mental aberration that leads a parent to imprison, physically abuse and starve a child is not merely a modern phenomenon. Here is an example from 1856, where the whole family seems to have colluded in the ill-treatment of one daughter.

Martha and her family lived in Stilton. Her father, Edward Crewe, had been born in Liverpool, and earned his living in Stilton as a master cooper. He had married a local woman, Maria Martin. They had had seven children, but Maria had died in 1843, probably whilst giving birth to their last daughter, Lucy, who died within a short time of her birth. Edward was left to raise their surviving children alone. Martha was five years old when she lost her mother; two years later her elder sister, Sarah, died of heart disease, at the age of only fourteen.

The family had therefore certainly endured sad troubles, of the sort that were unfortunately all too common in the mid-nineteenth century. It would appear that Edward was a deeply religious man, and that he ascribed his sufferings to the will of God. In his mind, God had punished him with the loss of his wife and daughter (and later with the deaths of two other children), and he believed that the family's destiny was entirely in God's hands. This, it would appear, relieved Edward of any sense of personal responsibility for his subsequent actions.

It is not uncommon in such complex, destructive family situations for there to be collusion in blaming the victim of the ill-treatment herself for the sufferings inflicted on her, and so it was in the Crewe family. Martha's father accused her of wanting more than her fair share of the food he provided to the family, and over time he and his other children began to punish her by withholding food from her. She lost weight and became painfully thin. Then, of course, they could not afford to let people discover what they had done, and so they shut her up in the house to prevent the neighbours seeing her.

Whether her two sisters, Rebecca (aged twenty) and Eliza (aged twenty-one) had any feelings of guilt or shame about their conduct, it is impossible to know.

The neighbours had heard Martha calling out 'Murder!' and crying out for food on almost a daily basis. They reported the matter to the parish authorities and the constable was sent to the house to investigate.

He found Martha at the cottage, miserable and thin. He asked her if she would like to leave the cottage and go with him, but she replied (in the presence of her sisters) that she wished to stay with the family. The constable therefore left them to it, but the family were offered free medicine for the girl, which was taken to the house. The father returned it unused, with what was described as 'a saucy note', in which he presumably told the authorities to mind their own business.

A neighbour, Mrs Smith, took some new laid eggs to the house for Martha one day, but her father refused to let her have them, and Mrs Smith had to take them home again. Mrs Wood, the innkeeper's wife, had once taken the girl some broth, but again the father had refused to let her have it. After this, Martha was not seen by anyone for more than two years.

On 18 August 1856, Martha managed to escape from the cottage. She ran to Mrs Smith's house and begged for help and for food, and was nearly in a state of collapse. The neighbour was very shocked at her emaciated appearance, but before she could do anything to help the girl, Rebecca and Eliza came running to the door and took hold of Martha and escorted her back home, saying that she was deceitful, and that she would suffer for her actions when her father was told about it. The parish authorities were called in again, and sent the constable back to the house to insist on seeing the girl for himself. What he saw was truly shocking.

Martha had been starved to the point where she was barely alive. Her bones were visible through her skin, and the constable described her as 'a living skeleton'. Her forearms were no thicker than two fingers, and she could scarcely stand. She was crying in pain; her bones protruded so much that she couldn't even lie down. She had suffered beatings. When asked why she never went outside to take any exercise, she replied that her father locked her shoes away.

There was a fierce physical struggle as the police tried to carry her out of the cottage, with the two sisters clinging to her to prevent her removal. Eventually, she was carried out and taken to the workhouse hospital, where medical attention was given. She was found to weigh just 56lbs – that is about 25 kilos. Her father and both of her sisters were arrested on a charge of imprisoning her, and of withholding food and clothing with the intent to murder her. The case was committed to the Lent assizes for trial.

Martha sadly died very shortly after her rescue, but had made a dying statement in which she said that her sisters had been responsible for most of her beatings. When she used to hold her hand out for food, her sisters would beat her arm away.

When the case came to trial, the medical evidence was that Martha had been suffering from scrofula. Scrofula was a type of tuberculosis that affected the lymph glands, and one symptom of the disease was weight loss. The doctor giving evidence at the trial said that another symptom was a 'morbid' craving for food. This is not supported by any scientific evidence available today, but her father complained that she had constantly wanted to be given food and that she could never be satisfied, no matter how much he gave her. He said that she had demanded food even when 'she had had bread in her pocket'. He claimed that he had suffered greatly on Martha's behalf.

As a result of the evidence that she had suffered from scrofula, the legal issue to be determined was reduced to one of illegal imprisonment, as it was not possible to determine that the starvation was what had led to her death. The jury were therefore only required to decide whether the imprisonment of the poor girl was from any motive other than to protect her, and they did not take long to find the father and both of the sisters guilty.

Edward, Rebecca and Eliza had already been held in prison for some 6 months by the time the case came to trial, and the judge sentenced the father to a further three months, and the sisters to a further one month each. It is difficult today to understand how such lenient sentences could have been contemplated for the years of deliberate suffering they caused.

In his summing-up, the judge said that the purpose of the prosecution was not to try to abate cruelty with more cruelty (i.e. by a stiff sentence), but to make the point that the head of the family was not permitted in law to mete out harsh or cruel treatment unless he could show that it was for the benefit of the person who received it. It is a rather shocking sign of the times, of course, that a man could be regarded as entitled to inflict cruel treatment on a member of his household 'for her own good'.

Edward Crewe served his sentence and returned to his home and business in Stilton, where he died on Christmas Eve in 1878, at the age of seventy-eight.

Martha's sister, Rebecca, was also said to have rarely been seen outside the family home. She never married, but kept house for her father for many years, before taking employment locally as a servant. Her brother, George, who had followed his father into the coopering business, left Stilton as a young man to go and live and work in Hulme, near Manchester. Rebecca seems to have followed him there after her father's death. She died there at the age of sixty-one, of heart disease. Her brother died of cancer in the workhouse at the age of fifty-nine.

Eliza remained in Stilton for the rest of her relatively short life, dying there at the age of thirty-one, of a condition involving fluid on the brain.

## Not just any eggs: Huntingdon, 1839

A labourer was convicted at Huntingdon assizes of stealing two eggs, and the judge was about to sentence him when an 'amicus curiae'[3] popped up in the court room and pointed out that the format of the indictment was bad: it should have specified that the eggs in question were the produce of two domestic fowls. The judge agreed, and the miscreant left, a free man.[xviii]

---

3 Amicus curiae: a person unconnected with the case but who assists the court with some information or expertise.

# Gaoling the gaoler: Henry Russell: Great Stukeley, March 1832

Henry Russell was the governor of Huntingdon gaol. He was responsible for the management and conduct of the prisoners, for the conduct of the staff, for the state of the prison finances and for the health and morale of the inmates. His was a position of enormous trust. His arrest on a charge of murder was, therefore, the last thing that anyone expected.

Sarah Wormsley was one of four sisters who lived with their father and mother in a cottage in St Peter's Lane, in Great Stukeley. Their house was only about 200 yards from the gaol, and Henry Russell and his wife were well known to the family. When she was about twenty, Sarah had gone to live-in as a servant at the Russell household. She had only stayed a few months, and had then returned to her parents' home.

The day before Sarah died, her sister, Lucy, had noticed Russell pass by the cottage several times, with what looked like a gun in his hand, staring hard into the interior of their cottage. The following day, both girls were at home when Russell slipped into the cottage garden surreptitiously, and took Sarah a little distance away to hold a private discussion lasting about ten minutes. Lucy noticed that Russell had something tightly clenched in his fist, and when he left, she overheard him say to Sarah that she must not let anyone know that he had been there.

The next day, the last of Sarah's life, Sarah had met her family for breakfast at about half-past six in the morning, and was obviously not well. She had been quite sick, and she gradually became worse. Her mother had gone outside with her daughter into the lane to hold her as she was repeatedly sick, and asked her if she had taken anything, but the girl said she had not. She noticed that Sarah was bringing up a thick, white chalky substance.

The mother had then sent for the turnkey's wife from the gaol to help her, and for the doctor. Sarah's face and eyes were very red and swollen, and she was in a cold sweat.

The doctor recognised the white substance as arsenic, and immediately contacted a magistrate to report his suspicions that she had been poisoned. The magistrate, Sir John Arundel, attended at the cottage and took a deathbed statement from Sarah. This is what she said:

*'Sometimes I think I shall die – sometimes think I shall not. I feel very ill. I was quite well when I got up his morning. I am with child. Before Michaelmas I felt with child, but I have not felt the child move. Between 7 and 8 this morning I took some arsenic – very near two teaspoons-full. I took it in some warm tea. Mr. Russell, the gaoler, gave me the arsenic yesterday afternoon. I lived with Mr. Russell as servant for 14 months. I left his service last Michaelmas. I had connexion with him several times. It is a year and a half ago since I first had to do with him, and from that time to this occasionally – not very often. I was never with child before. Last week I told Henry Russell I was with child. Henry Russell said it was a bad job: did not know what would be the consequence. I don't know anything else that did pass. I don't know how he came to give me the arsenic. He did not tell me the effect of it. He gave me nothing else. He gave me it yesterday afternoon. I did not know what the arsenic would do. He told me to take it, and I took it.'*

Henry Russell was fetched to hear the deathbed statement being read out, and was allowed to put questions to Sarah, though he said very little. Her suffering continued for several hours, and she died in the early evening.

The following day, a warrant was issued for Russell's arrest, and initially he was charged with her murder. He was remanded in Huntingdon gaol until his trial.

Sarah's mother said repeatedly that both Henry Russell and his wife had always treated her daughter very kindly whilst she had been in their service. So far as she had been aware, they had been like another father and mother to her. She said that their actions towards her daughter had always been humane.

She had noticed a change in her daughter some ten weeks or so before her death. Sarah had been engaged to be married to a local farmer's son, and her mother had suspected that she might be pregnant. Sarah had denied it when she had asked her, and it was not until her dying breaths that she had confessed to her mother that it was true, but of course the identity of the father could not have come as a greater surprise to the poor mother.

The doctor testified that no dose of arsenic was ever a safe dose. A single grain of arsenic could kill someone. The chemist who analysed Sarah's stomach contents reported that she had consumed at least sixty grains.

The trial naturally caused considerable local excitement. The irony of a governor of the gaol being incarcerated in his own prison meant that people from Huntingdon were queueing in the street from early in the morning in order to gain a seat in court. There was barely room to move.

Russell's indictment was now that he had been an accessory to Sarah's 'self-murder'. Suicide was, of course, then a crime, and the law provided that an accessory to any crime was subject to the same punishment as the principal wrong-doer. This approach to the issue of 'self-murder' was novel, and required some tricky handling by the prosecution, who needed to convince the jury that Sarah's actions made her guilty of a capital offence herself, and that Russell's part in the events had been sufficient to make him her accessory.

At the trial, the only evidence brought in Russell's favour were character testimonies. Everyone spoke of his great kindness and humanity, and of his being incapable of committing an unkind or improper act. He implored the jury to bear this in mind when weighing the evidence against him.

The jury deliberated for some time, and returned to say that they found it proved that Russell had given Sarah the arsenic in order to procure a miscarriage. The judge then told them that this meant that he must be found guilty. On that basis, the jury returned a guilty verdict, but it was clear that they had only done so because of the steer given to them by the judge on this technical point of law.

Russell asked the judge to spare his life, since it had never been his intention to take Sarah's. The sentence of death, however, was inevitable, because he stood convicted of assisting in 'self-murder'.

Russell was committed to his own gaol, to await execution. About a month after the trial, he was discovered to have been planning to make a break from the prison: a spike was missing from the fence round the exercise yard, and another stake had been deliberately loosened. If pulled away, it created a gap just big enough for someone to get through, and would have allowed him to get into the space just before the outer prison wall. Russell was found to be the author of these things because he had unwisely asked other prisoners to assist him in his escape. To add to his misery, therefore, he was now ordered to be kept in chains.[xix]

The law had not finished with him. Although the sentence of death had been passed, the judge did not send him for execution immediately, because his lawyers declared their intention of appealing against the sentence, on a point of law. That point of law came before a panel of thirteen judges at the Exchequer Chamber on 28 April that year. The legal arguments were very technical, but after hours of deliberation it was agreed that the King should be petitioned to spare Russell's life, on the basis that a sentence of transportation for fourteen years should replace the sentence of death.[xx]

He was put on board the *Parmelia* on 14 July 1832, and taken to New South Wales, where he was to begin a new, utterly alien life.

Many lives had been destroyed by the decision he had made to give Sarah the package of poison. At no time do we really hear his voice, with any explanation of his conduct. The jury believed he was trying to help her to cause a miscarriage, but no evidence was given that arsenic would do this, or that he believed that it would. He had a wife, and of course his affair with their servant was disgraceful, albeit sadly not unique. How was his wife to live after he had left? And Sarah's family, of course, were harrowed. They were a close family, and her mother had been so overcome with grief when she gave her evidence in court that she had fainted and had been unable to speak for several minutes.

15 *A scrimshaw depicting the convict ship Parmelia on which Henry Russell was transported.*

If we want to know a little more about Henry Russell, the man, the only help comes from the various character testimonies given at his trial. The words 'humane' and 'kind' were used repeatedly by many to describe him, including by Sarah's own mother, and even when she was in full possession of the facts as to how her daughter came to die, she still maintained this opinion of him.

Here are some of the things said about him at the trial:

Mr George Rust was a magistrate of the quarter sessions, and often conducted the quarterly prison inspections. He therefore knew Russell well. He spoke 'in the highest terms' of his kind and humane character.

Rev. Lee, the prison chaplain, had known Russell throughout the years that Russell had been in charge of the gaol. 'I had frequent opportunities of seeing the conduct of the prisoner, and his general conduct has been that of a humane, kind-hearted man.'

John Grant, governor of Northampton Gaol for the preceding fourteen years, said that Russell had been his assistant there for eleven years; for the first three of those he had been the prison miller and baker. 'I should say he was a man very incapable of doing an unkind or improper act.'

Further similar testimonies came from the deputy clerk of the peace, the surgeon of the county gaol and others.

It seems that the inmates of Huntingdon gaol lost an unusually good – if fatally flawed – governor. There must have been many a moment afterwards when Russell thought 'if only ...' If only he had behaved himself properly with Sarah; if only he had not tried to 'help' her to end the pregnancy; if only he had understood that the powder was lethal taken in such a dose. If only she had thrown it away and not taken it.

It is very rare indeed to be able to learn anything of the life of a transported convict at this period, but, remarkably, something of Henry Russell's life in New South Wales has survived.

It seems that, on arrival in New South Wales, his earlier skills as a miller and baker were identified, and he was placed on a cattle station called Castle Forbes, where he was miller for six months before becoming a watchman.

Castle Forbes was renowned as one of the finest cattle stations in the territory, but was also well known for something less creditable. It belonged to James Mudie, about whom much is known, and whose achievements were assisted by many convicts who were assigned to work for him.[xxi] Mudie was deeply feared by his men. He was a strict disciplinarian, and floggings were a regular occurrence, even for minor infractions.

In November 1833, six of the convicts working for Mudie rebelled against the regime at Castle Forbes by breaking out, stealing food from the stores and running away into the bush. They tried to shoot Mudie's deputy and son-in-law, Larnach, but they missed. The men were eventually arrested, and tried, and Henry Russell was one of those who gave evidence about the general conditions at the cattle station. His statement provides a really rare window into the personal experience of a transported convict, and also gives us a little satisfaction in knowing something of his existence after he left Huntingdon gaol:

> *I am assigned to Mr Larnach. I am a watchman[4] now. I was employed as a miller at Mr Mudie's for six months from Christmas last; I have ground good and bad wheat; I have ground tailings; the flour was the same used in the house as on the farm by the men; I recollect when the men complained to Mr Larnach of the flour, about eight months ago, the flour was changed in consequence of the complaint.*

---

4 A watchman was in charge of the safety and security of the cattle on a station. He would spend the night in a bothy or shed with the shepherd dogs to guard against predators.

*Since I left the mill there was bad flour served out once since, about four months ago, the men reported it again then, and Mr Larnach ordered it to be washed. I went up to the yard with the men, but I did not join in the complaining; I had no cause to find fault with the meat; we had inferior meat sometimes, but I know from the state of the country it was impossible to have it always good; when the men at the house were making complaints, my meat was very good; I was in the flats at the sheep station. I was punished twice: I was charged for not entering two bushels of wheat in the books, and I first got fifty lashes for that and was sent to work on the farm; the second was for allowing one of my own shepherds to come into my hut.*

*I was governor of the County Gaol and House of Correction at Huntingdon before I came out to this Colony. I was nearly five years in that situation; before I became Governor of Huntingdon gaol, I was ten years principal Clerk and Turnkey of Northampton Gaol. I often had four hundred prisoners in my charge at Northampton; I ought to be a good judge of the treatment of prisoners, I consider we are much better treated than prisoners are in gaols in England. I don't know what the Government regulations are; we get ten pounds of dressed flour [...] I got tobacco and sugar when I was at work, and pumpkins and melons and turnips; we were allowed to take them from the field; we were allowed [...] three cows to ourselves.*

*I never heard either Mr Mudie or Mr Larnach abuse their men. A beast was killed once a week, and I have known nineteen pigs killed once, the offal was given to the men in addition to their rations.*

*I came out to the Colony as accessory to a suicide; when I was flogged I thought I was hardly used; when I came to Court I expected to be punished, but I thought the last case a hard one; the men used to say they would get flogged right or wrong; those who had been punished used to say this; I never heard the well-behaved men say they would be punished right or wrong; on the last occasion I pleaded ignorance of the regulations being a new hand; I was told that was the reason I only got 12 lashes.*[xxii]

Russell may not have been a completely free agent in giving some of this testimony, because he was still working for Mr Mudie, whose regime at the cattle station was under severely critical scrutiny in this trial, and indeed for some years afterwards. However, what comes through is a man who was philosophical about his position: he accepted punishment when it was due, had an opinion as to whether it was fair or not but kept it to himself and

16 *View across Castle Forbes cattle station today. No doubt Russell would have appreciated being out at work in this landscape after being incarcerated in Huntingdon gaol.*

17 *Castle Forbes Ranch house.*

carried on with his work; he found the treatment of the convicts fair, and took the rough with the smooth. These qualities would, no doubt, have helped him to endure his exile.

## Incurring the wrath of the duchess: Mary Savage, Kimbolton 1897

Mary Savage was a lady of respectable birth, who had formerly been able to support herself on her own independent income. Unfortunately, she had fallen victim to a notorious financial scandal in 1892, and was then forced to work for her living.[5] In about 1893, she took employment as a housekeeper at Kimbolton Castle.

Technically, all the staff at Kimbolton Castle were employed by the trustees of the estate of the late duke of Manchester (the trustees being the dukes of Buccleuch and Abercorn), and not by the young duke himself, who was then under-age. The widowed duchess no longer lived at the castle herself, having removed to London, but the young duke treated the castle as his 'base' whenever he was 'down' from Cambridge. Thus, the duchess, whilst no doubt an influential voice at the castle, was not, herself, in charge of the staff.

Mary Savage did not enjoy a good relationship with the duchess, but for a long time the trustees appear to have been satisfied to allow her to continue in her post as housekeeper. Thus, the two women seem to have tortured one another for a long time before matters finally came to a head in 1897.

The duchess wrote to Mary Savage in May 1897, saying, 'I do not want any more lies or protestations from you ... I know your character very well. I have found out all about you.'

In June she wrote to Mary again, saying, 'I hope there will be no scenes at the Castle ... I understand you refuse to give out linen articles ... I want no more blustering on your part, or I shall take measures to stop it ... It has cost about £40 to recover the various things you have hidden away ... The

5 The fraud was perpetrated by directors of the 'Balfour Group' in 1892, which left thousands of investors penniless and resulted in the imprisonment for fourteen years of Mr Jabez Balfour, the founder of the business.

18 *Duchess of Manchester (portrait by John Singer Sargent, 1907).*

character which you gave from Lady Beauchamp is now in the hands the police.'[6]

Mary had by this time been given a month's notice of termination of her employment, and was working out her notice when, on 8 July, she received another letter from the duchess, saying, 'I am extremely annoyed about the thefts at the Castle. Of course, I know where the things are, but I shall not return until they are given back.' Notwithstanding this, the duchess did, in fact, return to the castle the very next day, 9 July, and Mary was given a written direction to have her bags packed and to be out of the castle by 7 p.m. The duchess fully intended to supervise her departure personally.

The duchess became convinced that Mary had packed more than she was entitled to. Mary was accused of having taken a gold medal, and the duchess insisted on having the trunks unpacked before witnesses. It was said that this created a scene of almost indescribable confusion, 'with everyone claiming something'[xxiii] from amongst the more than three hundred articles packed in the cases. In fact, a number of items belonging to the ducal estate were discovered in her luggage, including vases, linen and pictures.

Mary was arrested, and committed for trial at Cambridge assizes. At the hearing in the following November she pleaded not guilty. Evidence was brought on her behalf that she was owed a considerable amount of money by the young duke's trustees. The young duke was in the habit of turning up at the castle with his Cambridge friends, expecting to be fed and watered. Being

---

6 i.e. 'character reference'.

under-age, he had no personal control over the purse strings, and so Mary could not look to him to cover the cost of these visits. She therefore used to fork out for their victuals from her own pocket. She had asked for reimbursement from the trustees when she was given notice to leave, but they had refused to settle up with her. After hearing all the evidence (which unfortunately is not covered in any detail in the press reports), the court was satisfied that she had not committed theft, and dismissed the charges against her.[xxiv]

That was of course good news for Mary, but she was still in a disastrous position, personally. Her humiliation had been very public indeed, with reports of the case appearing in every county in the land, and she was without a reference to offer a future employer. She found it impossible to find further employment.

As a result, by 1899 she felt she had no choice but to turn the tables on the duchess, and take legal action against her for 'malicious prosecution'. In order to succeed, Mary needed to persuade the court that there had been no reasonable cause for the criminal proceedings the duchess had instituted against her in 1897.

In court, the various letters sent by the duchess were read out to demonstrate the depth of the hostility under which Mary had laboured. Added to this, of course, Mary could show that she had been completely exonerated in relation to the alleged crimes. However, her case was completely sunk when the judge asked her counsel whether or not there had been items in her luggage that did not belong to her. Her counsel had to concede that there had been, albeit apparently innocently.

On this basis, the judge ruled that it simply could not be said that there had been no reasonable cause for the original proceedings against her, and the case had to be dropped.

Unfortunately, it has not been possible to trace the fate of Mary after these events. It is possible that she either left the country to start afresh elsewhere, or else changed her name, in order to avoid the stigma of the court proceedings.

# Somersham alight: Thomas Savage, 1824

Farmers were terribly vulnerable to fire, and relied on the labourers and their families to a large degree for vigilance and for prompt assistance in the event of fire being discovered. Many farm workers lived in tied cottages on the farms where they worked, and were therefore often first on the scene in the event of an outbreak. The farmers were not the only victims if fire took hold: the labourers could lose their employment and their homes in a serious case.

Thomas Savage set fire to a barn belonging to Mr Martin Wellman, farmer in Somersham, in May of 1824. The fire got so out of control that it destroyed many homes and buildings before it could be extinguished.

The night before the fire, Thomas had met an acquaintance on the road in the village, and had told him that he felt like setting fire to something. He discussed which buildings would suit his purpose best, and gave his opinion that if he set fire to Mr Wellman's barn or Mrs Ibbett's house, the fire would be able to spread nicely to the shop of Mr Mast, a mercer, who held a large stock of tailoring fabrics. He asked the acquaintance if he would be prepared to give him a hand, passing all the valuables out of the houses, and if he would, neither of them would want for anything forever more.

Sure enough, that night at about two o'clock in the morning, fire was spotted by a brewer's assistant whose job it was to rise early to set the brewing afoot. He raised the alarm, but little could be done.

It was reported that 'nearly twenty' houses had been either burnt down or seriously damaged in the fire. The human misery caused by the loss of so many homes and possessions must have been appalling.

The following day, Thomas offered his friend some fabric to make 'a pretty suit': it seems he had looted the tailor's shop of seventy yards of cloth and some silk before the fire reached it.

Curiously, he appears to have acquired a conscience about his actions, because he voluntarily surrendered himself to the law and confessed to his crime. In accordance with usual practice in the case of a capital crime, but against Thomas's wishes, he was directed to plead 'not guilty' at his trial. In his defence, he said that he would never have thought of doing it if his acquaintance, Mr Woods, had not suggested it first. The jury did not believe him and did not even retire to consider, but convicted him immediately. He was sentenced to death, and there was to be no remission of his sentence.

The following is the report of the execution which took place on Mill Common on 18 December 1824:

*On Saturday, Thomas Savage, who was capitally convicted at the last Huntingdon assizes, of wilfully setting fire to premises at Somersham, underwent the infliction of the law. His behaviour throughout the awful scene was truly becoming. On his way to the fatal spot, he kneeled in the cart, rested his arms on his coffin, and continued, seemingly in constant prayer; when arrived at the place of execution, he mounted the scaffold with a firm step, told the surrounding spectators, that he was quite resigned, had no fear of death, and wished they all were as happy as he then was. He was twenty-two years of age, and was a native of Somersham.'*[xxv]

## Bythorn alight: September 1864

Farm fires were reported right across our county in most years of the nineteenth century, but there seems to have been a particular spate of 'incendiaries' (deliberate fire-raising) in the 1840s, suspected by some to have been caused by disaffected farm workers taking revenge for lowered wages. Others accused the supporters of the Corn Laws of creating a culture of belief in reduction in supply in order to keep up prices, and therefore wages: misguided farm workers thought that by destroying crops they could make the grain scarce, and thus make their jobs more valuable, in much the same way that the anti-reformers believed they could uphold the price of grain by blocking foreign imports.[xxvi]

Naturally, the police investigated all such fires, and there are many examples of attempts to bring a suspected fire-raiser to justice. If convicted, a culprit could, of course, expect a very harsh sentence: in the early part of the nineteenth century, sentences of death were not uncommon, or transportation for life. However, fixing guilt on an individual for this kind of crime – where it is done in a second but may go undiscovered long enough to enable a getaway – was notoriously difficult. Arson cases almost always depended on circumstantial evidence, usually consisting of a motive of revenge coupled with opportunity, and this was often insufficient for a jury to convict. Juries were mindful of the severe punishment that would follow a conviction, and not keen to rush to a conclusion of guilt unless the matter was really clear. The judge would often steer the jury to acquit where the evidence was purely circumstantial.

The earliest reported conflagration in Bythorn occurred on 12 November 1771, in which ten cottages were destroyed. No other details are available, but the loss of so many homes in one very small village would have caused great hardship.[xxvii]

In October 1848, a potential disaster at the farm of Mr George of Bythorn was narrowly averted by the efforts of the labourers on the farm, who rushed to extinguish the flames. Luckily there was no wind to fan the fire, and there was a plentiful supply of water close by to douse it. Some wheat was lost, but by no means all, and the flames were prevented from spreading to the buildings. So grateful was Mr George that he published his personal thanks to all who helped him, in the local press:

> *'FIRE AT BYTHORN. NEAR THRAPSTON. F. GEORGE begs offer his best THANKS to his neighbours and friends for the spirited manner in which they came forward, and the valuable ASSISTANCE rendered to him on that occasion – and in this a large share of the obligation is due to the Labourers, particularly the women, whose conduct was most praiseworthy.'* [xxviii]

Unfortunately, he was not so lucky on the next occasion.

It seems that the autumn of 1864 was another particularly troublesome time for farmers in our area. As far away as Glasgow it was being reported that:

> *For the last month, ever since the harvest has been ended, the inhabitants of Huntingdonshire, and that part of Cambridgeshire adjoining, have been kept in a perpetual state of terror from the numerous fires that have taken place, the greater number of which have been attributed to incendiaries. Hardly a night passes but an attempt is made to fire stacks of wheat, hay, and other farm produce; and a watch is constantly kept on many farms […] fires also are recorded as having taken place recently at Swavesey, Alconbury, and Warboys, great damage in each case having been done. On Tuesday night three fires were to be seen in different directions from the neighbourhood of St Ives.* [xxix]

In September 1864, a fire was started in one of Mr George's haystacks, and before anything could be done to avert disaster, the flames took hold and spread to every stack on the farm. Once these were alight, the fire spread to the barns and outbuildings, and before long it rampaged through the farm cottages, too.

By the end of the night, very sadly, this constituted one of the largest recorded farm fires in Huntingdonshire (but certainly not the last in Bythorn), and so considerable was the damage, that news of it spread all over the country.

That night, Mr George lost twelve wheat stacks, eight barley stacks, five bean stacks and two straw stacks; five barns full of barley, oil cake, beans and wheat; two stables, two cow sheds, two cattle sheds, three cart sheds and a carpenter's shop full of tools and implements; a pony, a hog and eleven heifers; and no fewer than nine labourers' cottages.[xxx] The tumult, fear and frenzy can scarcely be imagined.

By the end of the night, only one farm cottage was left standing and, bizarrely, that was a thatched cottage standing in the middle of the row, with every one of its neighbours burnt to the ground. It was said to have been 'a signal mark of Divine Providence'. A reporter from the Cambridge Independent Press visited the site nine days after the fire broke out, and reported that in places, it was still burning.[xxxi]

There were collections raised throughout the area in support of the families who lost everything that night.

In the aftermath of these events, information began to emerge about the movements of various of the villagers that evening, and suspicion fell on John (also called Peter) Pettit, a farm labourer who also happened to be the parish clerk.

He had spent several hours that evening in the public house in Bythorn (not named in the reports, and there were at least two at that time, the Shoulder of Mutton and the White Hart). He had, of course, been seen by many others there, including the landlady, and there were many testimonies to his having left when the inn closed just after ten o'clock that night. He had been seen walking home to Keyston, taking the most direct route which took him past Mr George's farm. The haystack that was set alight was close to the road on this route.

The ostler at the inn said that Pettit had told him that evening that Mr George owed him some money, and had commented that Mr George had rather too much corn on his farm.

The claim that he was owed money by the farmer was the result of an old complaint. Pettit had worked for Mr George about five years before, as a horse handler, at Mr George's other farm, Manchester Lodge, in Keyston. Unfortunately, he had fallen out with the farm bailiff for refusing to follow his orders concerning the management of the horses. As a result, he ceased to be employed at the farm, whether by reason of being given the sack or because he walked out was a matter on which the parties disagreed. The result of his leaving at that point in time had been rather unfortunate, because Mr George had promised him a bonus if he had remained in his employment until Michaelmas of the year in question. Terminating his employment meant that he failed to achieve his bonus, and this had seriously rankled with him.

In fact, Mr George had had some sympathy with John Pettit over these events, and having personally investigated the circumstances (and taking into account that the man's father had worked for him for many years, and Pettit himself had worked for him since boyhood), he had immediately offered to take him back on, provided he agreed to follow the bailiff's directions in future. Pettit refused. He would not work at Keyston. He said he would, however, work for Mr George on the Bythorn farm, provided he was given a cottage there. Mr George could not, or would not, oblige him, and from that day onward there was an awkwardness between them. In fact, in the few weeks leading up to the fire, Mr George testified that Pettit had been 'uniformly disrespectful' to him whenever they met one another in the village.

The police interviewed a number of witnesses, including Pettit. Pettit was asked what time he had left the inn on the night of the fire, and he said it must have been about half-past nine. He said he had been in bed by a quarter to ten. When it was put to him that so many people had said that he had not left until after ten, he steadfastly stuck to his story. The police were suspicious and arrested him on suspicion of arson.

One of the policemen actually timed the walk, at a very fast pace, between the public house and Pettit's cottage in Keyston, Bythorn, and confirmed that it could not possibly be accomplished in the time that Pettit said it had taken him to get home.

At the assizes, thirteen witnesses gave evidence that they had seen Pettit leave the inn just after ten, and that they had seen him on the road in the vicinity of the haystack.

In his defence, Pettit's counsel said that if he had been motivated by revenge, it would have been more likely that he would have set fire to the farm at Keyston than the one at Bythorn: all the more so, since his mother lived in one of the cottages that burnt down, and his own child was staying in that cottage on the night of the fire. Whilst this may not seem like a very sturdy defence, it was, in fact, enough to give the jury sufficient cause for doubt, and they acquitted him.[xxxii]

The culprit and cause of so much misery and loss was never, therefore, identified.

It is curious to note that on the very same page of the Cambridge Chronicle and Journal in which the report of this trial appeared, there was also reported the trial of a farmer from Easton, accused of no fewer than three instances of fire-raising: first, of setting fire to the barn of a farmer there named Parson; secondly of setting fire to Mr Mash's straw and one of his farm buildings; and thirdly of setting fire to a farm belonging to Mrs Ferriman. Just as in Pettit's case, the defendant was demonstrated to have given false information about one element of his activities on the relevant night, but the judge in this case, just as in Pettit's, stressed that this was not necessarily sufficient to prove that he was guilty of anything worse than telling a lie. The jury again acquitted.

19 *The White Hart Inn, Bythorn.*

# The depths of despair: James Wallis, Kimbolton 1883

Sometimes an everyday piece of bad luck can lead to something momentous.

James Wallis had been born in Little Chart in Kent, but had come to Kimbolton to take up the position of postmaster at Kimbolton. He married Adelaide Clark, herself the daughter of the previous postmaster at Kimbolton, and together they ran both the post office business and a stationery and fancy goods shop in the village. All seemed perfectly well with the couple, and they had six children together in the space of nine years.

Unfortunately, however, beneath the surface James was a tortured soul. The whole of the family's savings had been lost as a result of the dishonesty of a stockbroker whom he had trusted. The broker had absconded with over £900 of their money, and the loss of so much had weighed very heavily on his mind. In fact, the family did not seem to be in any immediate financial difficulty as far as anyone could tell, but the events had clearly taken their toll on his mental health.

Eventually, his health completely broke down as a result of this misfortune, to the point where his doctor had recommended that he take a holiday and get a change of air. He took himself off to Matlock, but it didn't heal his mind, and it became necessary to take on an assistant to help to run the post office. A young man named James Chislett joined the family at Kimbolton in about December 1882, and seems to have taken good care of the postmaster. Such was the concern about his state of mind that Mr Chislett even occasionally slept in James's room to keep an eye on him, when he was particularly unsettled. James said that he had not really had a sound night's sleep for several months: although his brain slipped into some kind of stupor at night, it was ever turbulent, and he could get no real rest.

On 28 January 1883, James had been particularly unwell. He had been depressed, and had prayed, and sung, and suffered from fainting fits. Mr Chislett had been extremely concerned about him.

On Sunday 11 February, Mr Chislett had accompanied James and some of the children on a walk through the village. James directed the children's attention particularly to the grave of their grandfather, Mr Clark. He said that they should look at it carefully, because he would be lying next to him in less than a week. 'Nonsense, papa!' replied Ernest, the eldest boy. 'Oh yes I shall, my dear,' said James.

20 *Kimbolton, Abt. 1900.*

On 13 February, Mr Chislett had the chilling experience of finding James kneeling in the passageway of the house, holding a kitchen knife into his own throat. Mr Chislett relieved him of the weapon, whereupon the unhappy man pulled a smaller knife out of his pocket and immediately tried again. Mr Chislett had to wrestle it from him.

On the night of 14 February, Mr Chislett decided to stay with his master overnight due to his disturbed state of mind. Ernest (aged nine), the baby (aged two), and two other children were all sleeping in the next room. Mrs Wallis slept downstairs on a couch in the sitting room, as she needed to be up early to attend to the mail. At this date, she was heavily pregnant with their seventh child, which was due any day.

Mr Chislett was awoken at about two in the morning by James returning to the bedroom and getting into bed: when Mr Chislett asked him where he had been, he said that he had been down to the kitchen to get some coffee and some bread and butter. The two men chatted for a few minutes, and then Mr Chislett dropped off to sleep again. The next thing he knew was that he heard screams coming from the bedroom next to theirs, and heard Mrs Wallis calling to him. He saw that James's bed was empty. Running towards the children's bedroom he came across James who cried out 'I've done it! I've done it! It's my Erny!' As he entered the children's room he could see that Ernest was lying face down on the floor, covered in blood. His throat had been cut. The baby, also bleeding from a gash on its neck, was being cradled in the arms of its mother. The two other children were huddled in the corner of the bed, terrified.

Poor Chislett hardly knew what to do first. He took James downstairs and left him in his wife's charge while he ran for medical help, but found the first doctor was not at home, and had to run for another. By the time he got back to the house, James was in a high state of excitement, and Mr Chislett had to run for the police sergeant, and a nurse, and also fetch poor Adelaide's mother. When the police took James away, Mr Chislett went with him to look after him. He certainly earned his wages that night.

When the police sergeant had arrived on the scene, James immediately confessed to having killed poor Ernest, and said he should be hanged for it. In front of them all, he tried to strangle himself.

He was taken to St Neots magistrates court later that day, and several times fell to his knees in front of the magistrates, clasping his hands, and crying out repeatedly during the proceedings, 'Oh my darling boy! Art thou happy? I know thou art in Heaven, and may I soon be with you!'

Although James was committed for trial on a charge of murder, he never stood trial. Instead, he was committed to Broadmoor mental asylum on the grounds of his insanity, and he died there nineteen years later, in 1912.

Life went on for Adelaide in Kimbolton, because she had to continue to earn a living to support her remaining family. It had been James who held the position of postmaster, but after these events the members of the inquest jury joined together in sympathy and wrote to the postmaster general, begging him to allow Adelaide to take over her husband's appointment. They said that she was well-qualified to manage the affairs of the post office, and praised her business sense and unfailing courtesy. The letter was countersigned by the Duke of Manchester, the vicar of Kimbolton, the village doctor and the headmaster of Kimbolton School. Evidently, the whole community wanted to support her through these appalling events.

She was duly appointed, and carried on the post office business for many years, and when she retired, the appointment passed to her unmarried daughter, Dora, who lived with her.

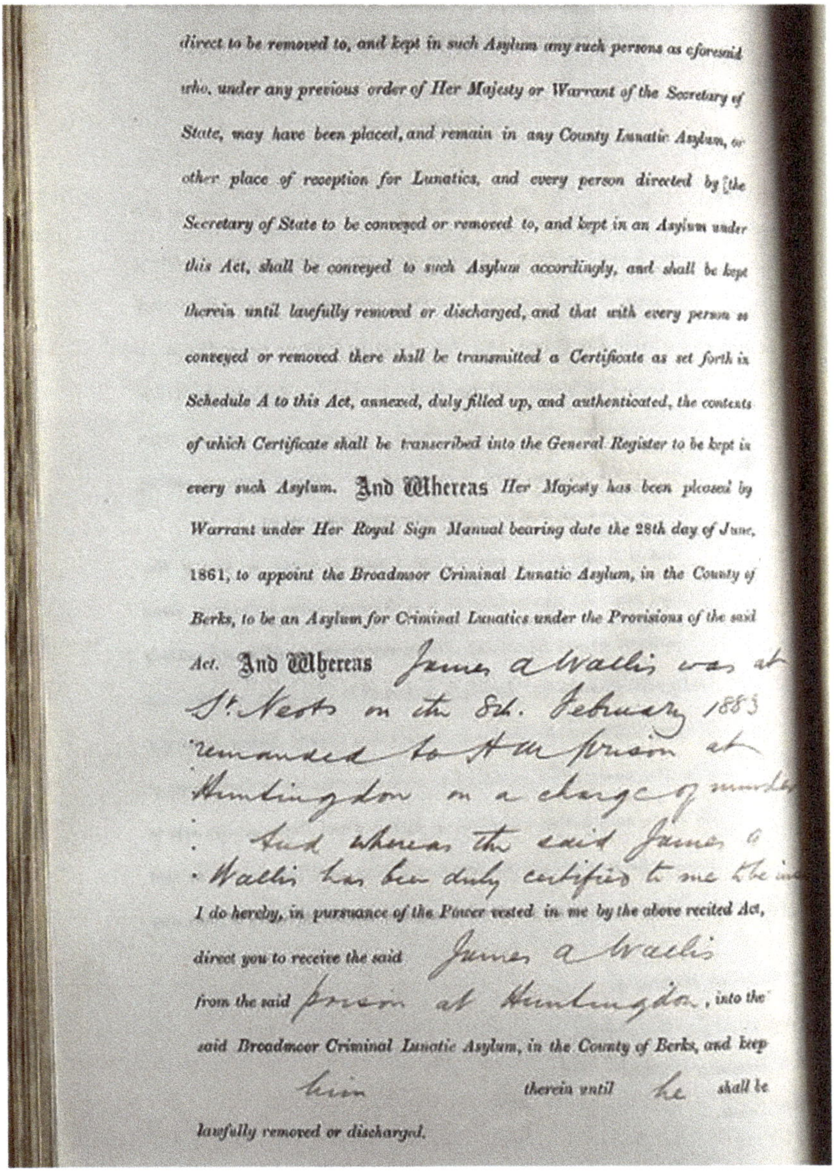
direct to be removed to, and kept in such Asylum any such persons as aforesaid who, under any previous order of Her Majesty or Warrant of the Secretary of State, may have been placed, and remain in any County Lunatic Asylum, or other place of reception for Lunatics, and every person directed by the Secretary of State to be conveyed or removed to, and kept in an Asylum under this Act, shall be conveyed to such Asylum accordingly, and shall be kept therein until lawfully removed or discharged, and that with every person so conveyed or removed there shall be transmitted a Certificate as set forth in Schedule A to this Act, annexed, duly filled up, and authenticated, the contents of which Certificate shall be transcribed into the General Register to be kept in every such Asylum. And Whereas Her Majesty has been pleased by Warrant under Her Royal Sign Manual bearing date the 28th day of June, 1861, to appoint the Broadmoor Criminal Lunatic Asylum, in the County of Berks, to be an Asylum for Criminal Lunatics under the Provisions of the said Act. And Whereas James a Wallis was at St. Neots on the 8th. February 1883 remanded to H M Prison at Huntingdon on a charge of murde

And whereas the said James a Wallis has been duly certified to me the in

I do hereby, in pursuance of the Power vested in me by the above recited Act, direct you to receive the said James a Wallis from the said Prison at Huntingdon, into the said Broadmoor Criminal Lunatic Asylum, in the County of Berks, and keep him therein until he shall be lawfully removed or discharged.

21 *James Wallis's order for committal to the Broadmoor.*

# Mr Hart: 'a substantial – nay, an opulent – farmer': Huntingdon, 1853

Miss Emma Jackson was the 18-year-old daughter of a well-known and respectable farmer in Cockayne Hatley. She brought an action for breach of promise of marriage against her former fiancé, Mr Hart. The newspaper reports of the trial coyly described her as 'possessing many personal attractions and a winning address'. Her own counsel described her as a simple, guileless and innocent young girl.

Her wealthy neighbour, Mr Hart, although twice her age, had apparently become overwhelmed by these personal charms, and in 1849 he spoke to her mother about making her daughter an offer of marriage. Mrs Jackson was content to permit it, subject to the girl's wishing it, and of course subject to her father's consent. Mr Jackson was a little more reticent, explaining that his lifestyle was just a little less opulent than Mr Hart's, and so he could not expect any fortune to come with his daughter's hand. It was good to be clear about such things.

Mr Hart let it be known that this was no obstacle to his feelings or intentions. Emma consented to his proposal, and the wedding was fixed for October in the following year, 1850.

When the date for the wedding approached, Mr Hart was unlucky enough to be struck by a serious fire at his farm, which caused him a great deal of upset and inconvenience. As a result (he said), he needed to postpone the wedding. The couple had been 'together' at this point for two years.

Another wedding day was fixed, for March 1852. Emma's father was very ill at the time. The family moved to St Neots, and in fact Mr Jackson died shortly after the revised date for the nuptials was fixed. To the family's surprise, Mr Hart absented himself from the funeral, and his visits to Emma ceased. As soon as it became clear that Emma would receive nothing from her father's estate, Mr Hart declined to go through with the marriage.

Less than one month later, Mr Hart married a wealthy cousin, much closer to his age. Emma began proceedings for breach of promise.

When the matter came to court, the court room was absolutely crammed with curious local people hoping to hear something sensational. They were not to be disappointed.

Emma's counsel, in relating the history of the couple's 'affair', played his audience (and the jury) very well. Having reached the point in the story where the first wedding date was postponed, he told them:

> *'And now comes the painful part of the case. Under the most solemn protestations of marriage and of affection towards this young and interesting lady, at a time when her father was in very indifferent circumstances, Mr Hart took advantage of his position, and completed her ruin.'*

The word 'sensation' appears in italics after these words in the newspaper report, and it is not difficult to imagine the delicious sharp intake of breath that occurred at this juncture. The sad truth was that poor Emma was pregnant, and in due course she gave birth to their child, a little boy, but he died soon after.

Emma's counsel contrasted the position she was now in, with the position in which she should have been: now ruined, and without prospects, instead of the virtuous wife of an 'opulent' gentleman. Now without any protector since the death of her father, it had been her friends who had supported her to bring the action against Mr Hart.

In defence of Mr Hart, his counsel needed first to try to discredit the claim of there ever having been any betrothal; next to discredit the notion that Emma had been disgracefully seduced by Mr Hart, and then to discount the suggestion that Emma was poor, or that his client was able to afford a large sum in compensation.

For the first, he could do nothing more convincing than point out that all the alleged references to the marriage had been made to members of Emma's family, and no independent witnesses had been called to prove the engagement. He didn't really expect the jury to fall for this, however, so he ploughed on.

He tried to deflect the awfulness of his client's having taken advantage of the girl by turning the tables, and pointing out that she had 'two years' experience of courtship' by the time of her 'seduction', hinting that she was as responsible as Hart for what went on between them. He did his best to suggest that she had trapped him, by pointing out that many seventeen-year-old English girls were more than a match for most men.

Finally, on the matter of the size of any compensation, he tried to catch the plaintiff's lawyer with his own hook: if Miss Jackson was so poor as was suggested, well, 'the daughter of the patrician must have more than the daughter of the peasant, and Miss Jackson was the daughter of a person with no property whatsoever.' This was nasty.

The jury considered their verdict for just fifteen minutes, and then awarded Emma what was, for those days, the relatively substantial sum of £500.[xxxiii]

## A tip for a lead thief: William Hunt, Godmanchester, 1865

Mr Thackeray was a plumber and glazier based in Godmanchester. Sixty pounds of lead bits and pieces went missing from his premises on 3 February 1865.

The next day, a labourer named William Hunt knocked on the door at the residence of police sergeant Bedlow, at Eaton Socon, and enquired whether he was in. The sergeant was brought to the door, and Hunt handed him a piece of lead pipe, saying that he had picked it up in the road between there and Buckden. He was just doing his civic duty in handing it in. The sergeant was very surprised to hear that such an item should have been lying in the road, and Hunt then embroidered the story by saying that it had probably come from a builder's cart that he had noticed going past. He gave the sergeant a false name, and said that he was on his way to Bedford in search of work.

Leaving the pipe with the sergeant, he asked him whether he could find him a little something for his trouble and honesty in handing it in. He must have been delighted to be rewarded with 6d.

It was not long before Sgt Bedlow realised his embarrassing mistake, however. He set off in hot pursuit of the man, and managed to overtake him at Perry. Hunt was charged with the theft, and he confessed. No doubt Sgt Bedlow was thereafter a little more cautious with his tips.

# Missing the warning signs: Jane Haynes, Tilbrook 1881

Thomas Richard Haynes was a corporal in the Royal Engineers. He had come to Tilbrook in about 1880 to take charge of an Ordnance Survey party in the area. Thomas's job would have involved overseeing a number of participants, from surveyors to labourers, in order to produce the updated Ordnance Survey maps of the 1880s that we find so useful and fascinating today. There were teams of Royal Engineers all over the country carrying out this work.

Thomas and his wife, Jane, had two children: a son named Thomas, who was about four, and a ten-month-old boy named George. They were regarded as a very close and loving couple. Unfortunately, however, Jane was finding it increasingly difficult to cope at home, and it did not escape the neighbours' attention that she was failing in her duties as a wife: the children were not kept clean, and meals were not being cooked.

She seems to have been suffering from a serious case of post-natal depression, although this did not then receive the recognition that we hope it would today. For a wife to fail to perform the duties of housewife and mother was regarded as quite shameful. It was said that the children were sometimes not washed for two days together, and that Thomas would return from a hard day's work to find that there was no hot dinner on the table for him.

Jane was alternately passionately affectionate towards little George, and at other times appeared quite insane and incapable of looking after him. Thomas was all too aware that she should not be left alone with the children during these difficult episodes.

Towards the end of October 1881, Dr Hallett of Kimbolton had been called to attend her, and had found this poor woman in the depths of despondency, saying that she didn't care whether she lived or died.

On 7 November, Jane's condition seemed particularly bad, and Thomas took the precaution of asking a neighbour, Mrs Gell, to take the children in, and care for them that day whilst he was at work.

Mrs Gell went to the house to fetch them, and found Jane wandering up and down the house saying that she was no kind of wife or mother, and she didn't understand why it was. The children stayed with Mrs Gell overnight, and were returned the next morning to Jane, who received them back very affectionately. She said that she would put little George down for a sleep.

Mrs Gell looked in on Jane again at about midday, and being unable to see

George anywhere about she asked Jane where he was. Jane said that he was still asleep.

When Thomas got home from work, Jane greeted him with the dreadful confession that she had killed him.

She took Thomas upstairs and showed him the baby lying on the floor with his throat cut, quite dead. 'He is better off now' she said. She later said that George was 'a little dear', and that she thought that the Devil had made her do it.

At her trial for murder, the jury were told that if they believed that Jane's state of mind meant that she was not aware of the nature of her act when she did it, it was not necessary for them even to consider whether she knew that her actions were wrong. It took them only a few moments to return a verdict of 'not guilty on the grounds of insanity'.

Jane was committed to Broadmoor Hospital 'during Her Majesty's pleasure'. She was just twenty-five when she entered Broadmoor. She remained there until her death, at the age of ninety.

It is not known when her husband died, but their elder son, Thomas, left England to settle in the United States in 1894, and became a naturalised American citizen. His father must have died before 1918, because in that year Thomas was drafted into the US Army, and he touchingly gave as his nearest relative his mother, care of Broadmoor Hospital.

At about Christmas time in 1922 he is known to have returned to England with the stated purpose of 'visiting relatives', by which we shall hope he meant that he went to see Jane, if he could.

## The Duke steps in: Freeman, farmer of Spaldwick, 1734

Masters had considerable control over their servants' lives and could punish them severely, and without interference from the law, for misdemeanours and infractions. It was considered to be in the interests of a servant to be 'corrected' in this way and an employer would need to do something quite egregious before the law would step in to impose any kind of limit. The following case is an example of something quite shocking that was, however, clearly felt by some to be borderline in its day.

*22 A view of Spaldwick, around 1910.*

A Spaldwick farmer named Freeman had a reputation for having a brutal temper. He employed a lad of thirteen, whose job one day was to take the farmer's cart through Kimbolton. Unfortunately, the boy accidentally overturned it.

Terrified of Mr Freeman's temper, the boy ran away, but his master had the advantage of being on horseback, and he soon caught up with him. He trussed the boy up with ropes, and then fastened him to the tail of his horse with a cord. Then, sitting astride his horse, he dragged the boy along the road, until eventually, the horse broke away and ran off, and the poor boy was found to be dead.

The farmer's story was that he was just about to give in to the boy's entreaties and release him, and was in the act of getting off the horse with his knife in his hand in order to cut him loose, when the horse had taken fright and had run off, with fatal results to the boy.

The jury at the coroner's inquest, rather surprisingly, found it to have been a case of accidental death.

Thankfully, it was not quite the end of the matter, because it came to the attention of the Duke of Manchester, near whose land this had occurred. He took a personal interest in the case when it came to his ears that Mr Freeman had, in fact, left the boy tied to the tail of his horse while he went into an alehouse, despite the boy being in desperate pain from his hands being too tightly tied up and crying out pitifully to be released. The man's only response had been to threaten the boy with even more punishment.

In his capacity as a magistrate, the Duke 'was pleased' to send for the farmer to come before him and, conducting his own investigation, he had the farmer committed to prison until the Lent assizes at Huntingdon.[xxxiv]

It was reported that, at the trial, it was 'proved' that the boy was 'an idle, untoward, wicked lad'. In this context, 'proved' simply means that evidence was given to that effect. The boy, of course, being dead, was not in a position to defend his reputation. The farmer was found guilty of manslaughter, but the sentence he received is not stated.[xxxv]

## Balancing the judicial with the extra-judicial: George Ward, October 1870, St. Neots

It seems that you could take young boys to church, but you could not make them pay attention to the service. No doubt it is quite different today.

In 1870, the Rev. G. B Watson, vicar of St Neots, was having a particularly bad time with young boys who behaved badly in the church. One must wonder what the parents were doing, to allow their offspring to cause a disturbance during divine service, but apparently the problem had been worsening over time. On 16 October there was a very nasty accident.

During the service, thirteen-year-old George Ward threw a piece of piping across the church, which unfortunately hit a young servant girl in the face. She had to receive medical attention for her injuries.

George was prosecuted for assault. He admitted he had thrown the pipe, but said that he had not meant to throw it at the girl, Mary Jane Townsend, in particular; he had simply 'chucked' it.

Rev. Watson seems to have felt badly about the boy being in court, and made a very feeling appeal to the court to be lenient with the boy, as he had no wish to see him punished severely. He said that he really was at his wits end with the behaviour of naughty boys in church. He wanted him punished, but leniently.

The bench fined George just five shillings, but they told his father to give him a sound flogging.[xxxvi]

# The Rev. George Tryon: Bringtown, 1857

In May of 1857, the Rev. George Tryon, a learned man and a mathematician, was appointed to the rectory of Brington, Old Weston and Bythorn. There appears to have been some legal technicality that rendered the appointment potentially invalid, and early in the June it was feared that the appointment would have to be brought before the ecclesiastical court to be decided. Eventually, he took up his new post towards the end of July. His tenure, however, was tragically short-lived.

He had taken some accommodation in Old Weston whilst the rectory in Brington was being refurbished for him. On Sunday, 26 July, he conducted his first – and sadly his last – service in his new parish, and one or two people noticed that he seemed a little odd in his behaviour.

On the morning of 28 July, he failed to appear at breakfast time. His servant tried to enter his bedroom, but found the door locked. In panic, he sent for the church warden, Mr King, who broke into the bedroom and found poor George Tryon lying in his bed in his night attire, with his throat cut, one hand still holding the razor with which he had dispatched himself.

23 *Old Weston.*

Suicide was, of course, not only regarded as a mortal sin, but was also a crime, and for a minister of the church to have committed such a shocking act was scandalous as well as tragic. There was no clue as to the reason for his disturbance of mind. So far as is known, the parishioners of Brington, Old Weston and Bythorn were not then, and are not now, especially noted for instilling terror into their minister.

## Miss Maule and Mr Fowler: Breach of promise of marriage, 1874

It was an unfortunate fact that in the nineteenth century, civil proceedings – including those between a man and his wife or fiancée – were held in open court. It meant that they were the subject of hungry attention by newspaper reporters and editors all over the country. Any particularly aggravated or sordid matrimonial dispute was voraciously taken up and transmitted to local papers throughout the land, with the consequence that matters which families would much have preferred to remain private, were aired in public.

The touching tale of Constance (known as 'Connie') Maule of Godmanchester and Thomas Fowler of Huntingdon was one such case that was read at the breakfast table of people as far apart as Bristol and Edinburgh. The Penny Illustrated newspaper referred to the case as 'another case of The Love that Lived—and Soon Died Out.'[xxxvii]

The story unfolded at the Huntingdon assizes at the end of July 1874, when Connie brought an action against her former fiancé, Thomas Fowler, for breach of his promise to marry her. The intended union would have joined together two old-established local legal families.

Connie's father, grandfather, great-grandfather and great-great-grandfather had all had respectable legal practices in the town and had all held the position of mayor of Huntingdon.

Thomas Fowler had been brought up from the age of three in the household of his uncle, William Fowler, also a solicitor of long-standing in Huntingdon, and his uncle's wife, Catherine Margetts. The Margetts family were also an old and distinguished local family. There was quite a lot of 'self-esteem' involved in this case.

Thomas worked in his uncle's law practice. In 1872 his uncle had died and

24 *The home of Thomas Fowler in High Street, Huntingdon.*

Thomas had taken it over. The business was carried on from the house where Thomas lived with his aunt, in the High Street in Huntingdon. By the date of the breach of promise proceedings, his Aunt Catherine was about sixty-three years of age, and she appears to have held all the cards so far as her nephew was concerned. She might have been the model on which P.G. Wodehouse based his character of Aunt Agatha.[7]

It may seem curious that a young man of thirty-four, with a professional practice in a thriving market town, should be entirely dependent on the goodwill of his aunt in all things domestic, financial and matrimonial, but such was apparently the case.

The Maule family had known Thomas since his childhood. Connie's father and Thomas's uncle were professional colleagues within yards of each other for many years in the High Street. In about August 1873, Thomas became an accepted and regular visitor to their family's home after several 'chance' meetings with the eighteen-year-old Connie and her sisters on the River Ouse.

7 Aunt Agatha ate broken bottles and wore barbed wire next to the skin. (The Code of the Woosters, P.G.Wodehouse, 1838).

The Maule girls were in the habit of rowing a boat about on the river that backed onto their home in Post Street in Godmanchester. It will come as no surprise to learn that Thomas was on the river because he was rowing his aunt about.

The newspaper reports suggested that before long, the regard that Connie and Thomas had for one another 'ripened into love', but whether that is actually the case or not the reader must judge from what ensued.

Time waxed, and Connie's father might have noticed the absence of any approach by Thomas for the traditional interview in which his intentions and his personal prospects would be discussed. Connie's brother, Henry, certainly noticed it, and so did Connie.

Henry, aged just twenty-three, took it upon himself – apparently without his father's knowledge – to drop Thomas a line of encouragement:

*26, Percy Circus, London*
*5 August 1873*

*Dear Fowler,*

*I dare say you will think is strange hearing from me, but I feel myself in duty bound, as a brother, to either see you or write to you: and I think that you, as a sensible man, will see that I have not gone too far. Have you, my dear Fowler, any serious intentions towards Connie? From what I have seen, I should say that you are either serious or else just amusing yourself. Anyhow, you are making the girl truly miserable, and the sooner you leave that sort of thing off the better; or, if, on the other hand, you mean anything serious, go at once, like a man, and speak to the governor. You will find him very fair and straightforward and, whatever answer he may give you, I am sure will be met in a most gentlemanly manner. But you can hardly expect that I, being her brother, and her eldest one, can stand by and see her looking so miserable without taking any notice of it – can you? And although I am so much your junior, I sincerely trust that you will take it in the same light as I send it. Hoping that you and yours are quite well, believe me, dear Fowler, yours very truly*

*H. St. J. Maule.*

It was a noble attempt on Henry's part, if a little misguided and naïve, for the letter could not be seen otherwise than as a slight to Thomas: either he had toyed with Connie's affections, in which case it was not the behaviour of a gentleman, or else his intentions were honourable but he needed this much younger man to tell him how to get on with the job. There really was no upside to the position in which Harry had placed Thomas Fowler.

It was therefore entirely predictable that Thomas would respond with a deft put-down:

> *My dear Harry,*
>
> *Your letter has surprised me in many ways.*
>
> *Your inexperience, coupled with my regard for your family and yourself, prevent my regarding what I should regard from any other than you an unwarrantable insult. I hope you will give your time to your studies, and pass your forthcoming examination with success to yourself and gratification to your friends, and leave Connie and me to take care of ourselves, or rather me to take of myself and your father and mother to take care of your sister . . .*

Harry kept this correspondence a secret from his father, but he did show it to his mother. She wrote to Thomas Fowler asking him to meet her privately, and on 11 August they had a discussion during which Thomas told Mrs Maule that he loved Connie and wished to make her his wife.

Mrs Maule was a little cautious in accepting this avowal of love for her daughter, because she had heard rumours that Thomas's affections had been bestowed elsewhere: by a very curious coincidence, his name had been 'linked' with another Miss Maule, in Brighton. No allusion was made in the press reports to the coincidence of the names of the two young women, and it was probably taken for granted that they were not connected. Resources available to us today make it possible to determine, however, that the two Miss Maules were related very distantly, though one would have to go back to the sixteenth century to find their common ancestor.

Thomas was quick to assure Mrs Maule that it was all over with the other Miss Maule, as she simply didn't suit him at all. He told her that his aunt had said to him '*Why not go in for one of Edward Maule's daughters? That pretty, amiable one?*' and that he had replied that she was not pretty, but that she was amiable. He told his aunt that if she liked the girl then he would make her an offer. If he was trying to recommend himself to the girl's mother, this was rather a peculiar way to do it.

Connie's father had at first objected to the difference in their ages, and to the fact that his daughter and Thomas would be required to live with Thomas's Aunt Catherine. He did not consider that likely to be conducive to marital happiness. On being assured by the couple that they did not find these matters insuperable, he had consented to the match, but pointed out that having had fifteen children (eleven of whom were still living), he was not in a position to settle any money on Connie. According to Connie's father, Thomas told him that he had a fair business of his own, and that it would expand, and that his aunt had made a will settling her wealth on him. The lack of a fortune for Connie was, therefore, no obstacle.

Mr and Mrs Maule had then paid the expected 'duty visit' to Aunt Catherine, who was regarded as in loco parentis to Thomas. Having done so, however, they made no further attempts to cement any relationship with her, and no more visits were made. Catherine took severe umbrage at their coolness.

The engaged couple had carried on what was regarded as 'the usual affectionate correspondence' at first, but no date for the marriage was fixed. Aunt Catherine clearly became increasingly antipathetic towards the Maule family. She took Thomas with her on a visit to the home of the other Maule family in Brighton, where the first Miss Maule was still residing and was still unattached, and she let it be known to Thomas that her approval to the match with Connie was withdrawn.

Thomas does not appear to have been able to contemplate life without his aunt's approval. Whether his feelings for Connie had actually changed or not is a matter of speculation. He wrote to Connie to tell her that his love for her had not diminished, but that without his aunt's financial support for the marriage, it was impossible. Aunt Catherine herself wrote to Mr and Mrs Maule, informing them that she regretted the engagement, did not consider that it could make either party happy, and had not been aware when she 'consented' to it (Thomas was thirty-three!) that Connie was one of eleven children, and penniless.

The engagement was over. Nevertheless, Connie was not able to bring an action for breach of promise until a sufficient length of time had passed for her to be able to prove that Thomas had no intention of performing the marriage. This, of course, placed her in a very miserable position: she was no longer betrothed, but must continue to behave as if she was, for long enough to show that the breach was all on his side. She was unable to attend parties or dances, and could not begin to consider any other potential suitor.

Connie's father instructed a firm of solicitors from Grays Inn to present his daughter's case, and took the precaution of retaining not one, but two QCs[8]. Thomas instructed Baxter, Rose & Norton – the forerunners of today's leading city firm of Norton Rose. One must suppose that his aunt footed the bill, for they were one of the highest-profile firms in the country, numbering prime minister Benjamin Disraeli among their clients. This assemblage of legal heavyweights gives some idea of the importance to the parties of the outcome of the case in terms of their respective reputations.

Mr Maule's account of the conversation he had had with Thomas about his prospects differed from Thomas's, in relation to the somewhat important detail of Thomas's income. Mr Maule said Thomas had told him his income was £600 a year. Thomas said he had given it as £500 a year, but that out of this he had to pay his aunt rent for his office space and other expenses, leaving him with just £120 a year in his pocket. In 1874, an income of £120 for a professional man was very little indeed. It is very likely that he was exaggerating his poverty, but, equally, to have his personal finances reported in the newspapers for his local professional colleagues to gloat over would have been very embarrassing.

In the end, Thomas dropped his claim that there never had been any engagement at all, and so it all came down to the amount of damages to be awarded to the disappointed bride.

The judge commented that during the hearing, Thomas displayed 'a degree of acuteness and intelligence and self-possession that is rarely equalled and possibly never excelled.' [xxxviii] In other words, he would have known exactly what he was doing where money was concerned. They could assume that he had gone into the engagement fully aware that he was taking a young woman with no financial settlement of her own. The judge put it to the jury that the long and short of it was that Aunt Catherine told him he must choose between Connie Maule and herself (and the prospects she represented) – and he decided to take his chance with the aunt who held the purse strings.

The judge also reminded the jury that they were not awarding damages against the aunt, even if they suspected that the money to pay the damages would in fact be coming out of her pocket. They must only consider Thomas's own financial prospects when considering how to value Connie's loss.

---

8 A 'QC' is a Queen's Counsel: a senior barrister who has been specifically appointed by the Crown on the basis of merit.

The jury awarded Connie the sum of £1,250, which was a significant award for those days. No doubt, despite the judge's remarks, it was designed to pinch Aunt Catherine just as much as her nephew.[xxxix]

The end of the affair represented a degree of public humiliation and exposure of private details from which it would have taken both families – especially Connie – a long time to recover. It is difficult to appreciate how awkward professional life would have been for Thomas and Edward whilst this was going on (and afterwards), as they would not have been able to practice in the town in isolation from one another.

There was a happy ending.

About three years later, Connie went on to marry Charles Desborough of Hartford House in Huntingdon. The wedding was reported in the local newspapers with great excitement – there were seven bridesmaids, the path up to the church was carpeted for the bride, the event was attended by the Countess of Sandwich and numerous other noble and respected guests, the mayor lent them the Town Hall for the reception, flags were hoisted in Godmanchester and a grand ball was held in the town. Best of all, the groom was said to be especially loved and respected in the locality for his great kindliness, which was demonstrated by some of the gifts they received. They were given a cruet stand 'from the poor of Hartford', and a silver bracelet 'from the poor of Godmanchester' (worn by Connie at her wedding): that the

25 *Hartford House, Huntingdon, Connie Maule's eventual home.*

poorest people of these two towns wanted to spare what little they had to demonstrate their affection for the couple says much.

In return, 'with his wonted liberality and kindly feeling', Charles Desborough gave a generous quantity of meat and groceries to the poor cottagers of the town to enable them to celebrate his wedding day.

The couple went on to have six children, all of whom flourished.

Thomas Fowler did not marry the 'other' Miss Maule. He married instead a Fenstanton girl, named Annie Coote, the daughter of a coal merchant, nearly five years after deserting Connie. Annie had to move in with Aunt Catherine, so it is to be hoped she had a strong constitution. The couple had one son, Thomas, who went to Harrow and Cambridge. Sadly, he died in 1915, at the age of 35, possibly of wounds sustained during the Great War. Aunt Catherine died in 1890 at the age of 79, almost penniless.

## Maiden Assizes

It occasionally happened that the court of assizes and its retinue would arrive in town in all its glory, only to find that it had absolutely nothing to do. These occasions were termed 'maiden assizes', and by historic custom on such occasions, the judge would be presented with a pair of white gloves. This occurred in Huntingdon on several occasions during the nineteenth century, and on each occasion the judge would congratulate the local constabulary and the justices of the peace on keeping such good order in the county.

In 1883 there was but a single prisoner at the Lent assizes, and the judge commented that 'Huntingdonshire might be considered the premier county' for its maintenance of a law-abiding populace.[xl]

# Making off with Mary: Frederick Barratt and Mary Ellis, Somersham, 1840

By the date of these events, a piece of legislation known as 'Lord Lansdowne's Act' had been passed in 1828 specifically to deal with the abduction of an heiress for the purpose of 'marrying her money'. That such an enactment was needed says much about the times, and in fact this Act brought together several earlier pieces of legislation that tended towards the same effect. Marriage by this date required the consent of the woman, otherwise it was not legally effective, and so her money would have been safe, even if the abductee and her reputation were not. A forcible 'marriage' would not have led to any legal entitlement to the woman's fortune, but any chance that she might subsequently be able to make an advantageous match would, of course, have evaporated. Anyone found guilty of taking away or detaining an heiress against her will, with the intention of marrying her or defiling her for 'motives of lucre', was liable to be transported for a minimum period of seven years and a maximum period of life. The stakes were thus set intentionally high.

Mary Ellis of Peterborough was born in about 1823, the youngest of several children, and was the great niece of a wealthy farmer, John Whitwell of Werrington. Mary's own father had died when she was about a year old, and she had been brought up by her mother, Sarah. Under the terms of her great uncle's will, Mary stood to inherit about £4000 when she was of age.

Mary had been sent to a private school in Stamford, run by a Mrs Wilson. No doubt her mother considered that she would be quite safe in such a genteel environment, but there was unfortunately a viper in the nest, in the form of the music master, Mr Frederick Barratt. Mary received singing and music lessons from Mr Barratt, but some shocking secret extra-curricular activity began to occur during 1839 (when Mary was still just fifteen). Mary appeared to admit that she had initiated their interaction by laying a bet with him one evening (about what, we do not know), the stake being a pair of gloves. Mary having lost the bet, she presented her gloves to Mr Barratt the following day. Mr Barratt at that time refused the gloves, on the grounds that to accept them would have been quite improper.

However, one evening during a school trip to the theatre in Stamford it would appear that he had second thoughts. When the lights were turned down for the greater dramatic effect of a conjuring act by Monsieur Testot, the clown, Mr Barratt took the opportunity of putting his arm round her waist and telling her that he had given the matter of the gloves some more thought, and perhaps he should have accepted them after all. Despite the fact that Mrs Wilson was sitting next to him, he tried to give Mary a kiss, and she did very little to stop him.

The pair formed an ardent attachment to one another, which became known to Mary's family during the summer holiday of that year. Mr Barratt had been invited to her mother's house to give her music lessons; he had given her a ring, and the couple discussed when she should tell her family of their engagement. When it was discovered, it met with trenchant objections.

Mrs Ellis removed Mary from Mrs Wilson's establishment immediately, as we can well understand, and sent her instead to Miss Pocock's school in Somersham. No doubt Miss Pocock was told the reason why and her aid enlisted in keeping the wayward Mary on the straight and narrow. Miss Pocock however, fared no better than Mrs Wilson.

Mary somehow managed to see Mr Barratt once whilst she was at Somersham, but was then forced to write to her lover and hand him the mitten. This was what she was made to write to him:

> *Dear Sir,*
>
> *By the earnest entreaty and advice of my friends, and from my own conviction of its being the right path for me to pursue, I am induced to write to you, to say our correspondence and intimacy must now cease for ever. You are well aware that it has always been contrary to the wishes of my friends and best advisers, and my own judgment tells me that I could have no happiness in living under their displeasure. Their firm determination, I find, is to discard me entirely from their homes and affections – they have left me but two alternatives, and it would make me miserable to be unfriendly with my nearest and dearest relations. I hope you will consider this decisive, for I am firmly resolved to abide by my present determination.*

As soon as she was alone she wrote him a quite different letter, which (as it was put in court) was not presented to her school mistress for inspection:

> *My dear Mr. Barratt,*
>
> *If I may be allowed to address you so familiarly, for 'Sir' is very cold; in fact, I cannot bear it ... When you came to Somersham, you no doubt recollect a person passing through the yard: it was an old servant of Miss Pocock's: she recognised me, and two days after the school commenced she told Miss P., who, of course, told me she knew, and that they intended to write to my friends. I received a letter from them some days after, with nearly these words, saying that they left me this for my choice: my own dear friends and home, or to continue my acquaintance with you; if so, they intended to banish me for ever from their home. Now, you well know it was impossible for me to do that, as I am so young: if had been older, I should have acted very different ... it is my full determination never to marry. Perhaps you may smile, but I can assure you I am sincere; and, though this is the last time I shall ever address you, think not that I can ever forget one whom I so highly esteem. If possible, you will be more in my thoughts than before; and to God, who alone knows, my prayers will always be offered up for your happiness and welfare, and I hope, with his assistance, I shall be able to bear all this with fortitude ... I have one favour to ask you, and I hope you will comply, as it will be the last perhaps for ever; that is, that you will never pass me in Peterboro' or any other place you may meet me in without speaking to me. This may be an improper request; but if you did, no words could express my feelings: I think it would almost kill me. I must beg of you to excuse this being written in pencil, for I dare not be seen with a pen and ink in my hand ...*

So, from this we know that the twenty-five-year-old Barratt had pursued the teenager despite knowing that her family objected to his suit, and the girl had defied them all by permitting a further clandestine meeting with him.

On 3 March 1840, Mary was out walking with the school, and was at the front of the crocodile in company with Miss Pocock's younger sister, who was another pupil at the school. Suddenly, the girls saw a horse-drawn gig approaching them, in which sat Mr Barratt and another man and, before

Mary knew what was happening, Barratt jumped out, grasped her round the waist and hoisted her up into the carriage. Several witnesses from the school and from the village confirmed that she resisted and screamed out for help, but Barratt covered her mouth with a handkerchief and told her to keep quiet. He placed her between himself and the other man (the ostler from the Rose & Crown in Somersham), placed his knee across her to keep her from struggling out of the gig and made off with her, at top speed.

Mary's mother was dying at this time, and Barratt initially told her that he would take her home to her mother's house, and on hearing this she relaxed somewhat, as the carriage headed in the direction of St Ives (with the blinds pulled down), where they dropped the ostler off, and then Barratt took himself and Mary towards Huntingdon, and the Fountain Inn. Here, he told her that he had ordered a chaise to take them to Peterborough, but once she had got inside it she overheard the landlady tell Barratt that it was twenty-three miles to Thrapston – at which point she realised that they were not, in fact destined for Peterborough at all, and challenged him. He drew and cocked a pistol: Mary thought he was going to shoot her, but he told her that his intention was to marry her. If she refused, he said, he would be ruined, he would face prosecution, and would, in fact, shoot himself.

They changed horses when they got to Thrapston, but Mary held her tongue and did not raise the alarm. They got to the Hind Inn at Wellingborough, and here she thought she knew the landlord to be a Mr Billing, but on finding that the Inn was now kept by someone she did not know she decided against spilling the beans, and once again kept quiet. Then, she finally made him understand that she could not go with him, and entreated Barratt to take her to her brother's house at Northampton. Barratt, realising that it was all up, begged her to let him get as far as the train station at Weedon, so that he could make good his escape. Mary's brother had been alerted to the escapade and was, in fact, in hot pursuit of the couple, and finally overtook them at Weedon where he reclaimed the unfortunate heiress.

Very sadly, Mary's mother died two days after these events.

The trustees of Mary's inheritance lost no time in prosecuting Mr Barratt for the abduction. In court, Barratt's lawyers cross-examined Mary for nearly five hours in an attempt to paint a picture of mutual affection having led to a mutual plan to elope and marry. Mary, whether as a result of pressure from her family or in genuine anger at her abduction, made no attempt to deny their engagement but strenuously denied being complicit in the elopement.

The jury had to decide whether Barratt had run away with Mary for her money. In his defence, his counsel told the jury that this was an unsustainable allegation, because Mary had no money at that point, and he would have had to wait several years for her to come into her inheritance. In the meantime, apparently, he was able to earn a 'handsome income' from his profession as a music master. Just how 'handsome' his income was from this source we will find out a little later on. However, the jury were reminded of the extremely harsh penalty that he would suffer if they found money to have been his motive, and of course Mary had been painstakingly cross-examined as to the many tokens of her love that had been exchanged during their secret engagement. Perhaps not surprisingly, therefore, the jury found him not guilty of having abducted her for her money, but they did find him guilty of assault.

Barratt was sentenced to fifteen months' imprisonment, which he spent in Huntingdon gaol. The judge made the interesting comment that, as Barratt had not altogether forfeited the character of a gentleman, he would not add hard labour to his sentence.

This 'gentleman', incidentally, had told the poor ostler who provided the gig and horses that he was a policeman on official government business, on a mission to collect a certain young lady, and that he (the ostler) was required to come along in order to render assistance to the law – for which he would be paid at the rate of thirty shillings a day. In court, the ostler pointed out that he had never received his stipend.

It would be satisfying to know what happened to Mary after these events, but unfortunately the trail goes cold. One would imagine that after serving a prison sentence of fifteen months for the grossest abuse of trust on the part of this teacher, and given that he became bankrupt (and was immediately further imprisoned for debt) shortly after these events, he would find it impossible to gain a position at a school, and few parents would be willing to provide him with private pupils. His marriage prospects would, surely, have taken a knock, too. And yet, one would be mistaken.

Frederick Barratt married another of his pupils, Miss Elizabeth Stredder, in 1845. At that time, he was described as being a teacher of music in Stamford, so he had clearly returned without a blush to Stamford after his imprisonment and bankruptcy. Like Mary, Elizabeth was ten years his junior. She went on to provide him with eight sons and four daughters, but the course of their lives did not run entirely smoothly. Barratt's 'handsome income' was simply not handsome enough, and he was imprisoned in Lincoln Castle goal for debt once more in 1851. Again in 1854 Barratt was insolvent and made bankrupt, and probably imprisoned for debt. Once more in 1867 his debts overwhelmed him and this man – who could not possibly have had his eye on Mary's money because he had no need of it – was made bankrupt. Elizabeth died in 1876 when her youngest child was seven years old, and the difficulties she must have endured protecting twelve children from the workhouse through these tribulations can only be imagined. Two years later, Frederick remarried, and by this time referred to himself variously as a pianist and as a professor of music.

It would appear that for a man, kidnapping and seducing a pupil, serial bankruptcy and imprisonment, were no bar to a respectable career and family life.

Barratt died in Peterborough in 1886.

# Church and Chapel

The tension between nonconformists and adherents of the established church was felt all over the country in the seventeenth to nineteenth centuries, and it sometimes caused sharp divisions within communities. Our own rural villages were no exception.

By the middle of the nineteenth century, nonconformists had an increasingly important political voice, but they remained very sensitive to any hint of prejudicial treatment. They were quick to call it out where they perceived it, and the following are local examples – not trials by jury, but by public opinion.

## The 'Parson's Bench': the struggle to get a balanced bench in Huntingdon.

The clergy represented a significant proportion of any local bench of magistrates, leading to the accusation that the established church had an effective stranglehold on the magistracy. It was proving very difficult for otherwise respectable and upstanding nonconformist citizens to obtain appointment in Huntingdon, because its lord lieutenant would never put forward to the Lord Chancellor's office the names of anyone whose religious or political views were at odds with his own.

Mr Arthur Arnold was a radical liberal who, at the date of the following letter, had been recently disappointed in his attempt to become member of parliament for Huntingdon. He and his wife were particularly active in support of women's suffrage.

Mr Arnold wrote to the Lord Chancellor, asking whether he would consider a little 'positive discrimination' to even up the stakes. His initial letter received an official rebuff, but he wrote again on 9 January 1874:

*My Lord,*

*In addressing your lordship upon the alleged exclusion of Nonconformists from the commission of the peace for the county of Huntingdon, I was careful to state that I did not ask your intervention [. . .] I gather that though you are not disposed under the immediate circumstances to exercise your official powers [. . .] for the addition of names to the commission of the peace, your lordship does not regard with indifference the complaint made, on the part, it is said, of one-half the people in the county of Huntingdon, to the effect that highly-qualified persons are excluded from the magistracy because their political or religious views are obnoxious to the Lord Lieutenant, although, as I am informed upon the same authority, there is a frequent delay of justice owing to a want of magistrates. I feel sure that the Nonconformists of Huntingdonshire will for the present rest satisfied with the strong expression of public and personal opinion which has been evoked – an expression which they may reasonably expect must tend to promote the equitable exercise of the powers of the lord lieutenancy.*

*I am, my lord, your faithful servant,*
*Arthur Arnold.'*[xli]

26 *Arthur Arnold.*

27 *Winwick Union Chapel.*

## A slur on the character of Rev. W. H. Disney: Winwick, 1889.

The Rev. Disney was rector of All Saints Church in Winwick. In November of 1889 he was severely upset by the publication of what he regarded as quite scurrilous accusations about him by the pastor of the union chapel in the village, who rejoiced in the name of 'Snitch'.

Mr Snitch had published his accusations at the beginning of November, in the Northampton Mercury, but Rev. Disney had apparently missed it.[xlii] Hoping, no doubt, to stir up an exciting clerical dispute for its readership, the Mercury took the step of sending him a copy. They must have been pleased with the result.

There had been a long-running discussion nationally about the cost to poor labourers of renting allotment land, relied upon by them to grow enough food to feed their families. Rents had been rising, and various local allotment societies in the region came together for a meeting in Kettering to discuss their options. The thrust of their intentions was that they felt allotments should be under the control of parish councils, and not in the hands of the clergy, who could impose 'unreasonable' conditions.

Mr Snitch said that he wished them to hear a disgraceful story which would illustrate the worst excesses of the established church in relation to this issue: he read out the following extract from the minute book of the Winwick Chapel, which had been made by the previous minister, Mr French, in 1873:

> *One principal feature of this meeting was that of indignation, on account of the ungentlemanly conduct of the Vicar of Winwick [...], who on Friday, 27th January this year, visited several of the villagers, and sent messages to them, telling them that unless they took their children from the Chapel Sunday school, and sent them to the one he had just opened, he would eject them from their allotments [...] they must either forfeit their labour or their religious principles.*

Mr Snitch said that he was thankful to say that all the chapel members who rented allotment ground had chosen to uphold their religious principles, but that they had been served with written notices to quit as a result.

It was reported that this was greeted by many cries of 'Shame!'

Mr Snitch went further. In tear-jerking terms, he regaled the meeting with the tale of how one of these dispossessed allotment-holders had subsequently nearly starved to death. He never knew a better man. He was a man of steel. But Mr Snitch had had to spend his own money to support him for weeks on end or see him die of starvation. (Further cries of 'Shame!')

Another story was of a widow who had 'defected' to him shortly after his arrival as pastor at Winwick. First the widow had gone over to 'Chapel', and then, by and by, her sons had followed her and had begun to attend the chapel Sunday school. The Rev. Disney's wife had gone to see the widow's daughter and had warned her that she must surely know the condition on which the widow's allotment was let to her: if she did not make her sons attend the church Sunday school, the allotment would be taken away from her. (More cries of 'Shame!')

The final nail in Rev. Disney's coffin was that Mr Snitch had just that week encountered a hungry young Winwick lad in Peterborough, who was on his way to enlist as a soldier. Because his family's allotment was gone, he had no choice but to 'hire himself out to murder folks!' (And again, cries of 'Shame!')

Rev. Disney was stung. At the end of November, he penned his response. He described the article as unjust, untrue, slanderous and 'clap-trap'.

He said that the 'poor widow' had had her allowance stopped by the Guardians of the Poor for reasons which were well known in the village, and which (though he did not repeat them) would rather change people's opinion of her if they knew what those reasons were. Despite this, he had allowed her to keep her allotment. When one of her sons had then behaved particularly badly in school, and she had 'upheld her son in his impertinence', he had then finally taken the allotment away from her. It was after this that she left the church and joined the chapel, not the other way round.

He said that he had never heard of any poor man reduced to starvation in the village; he was sure that he would have known of any such case given that it was a very small village, and he had always made it his business to help the poor of his parish. He also pointed out that the Guardians of the Poor would never have let such a thing occur.

He had also never heard of the boy who went to enlist as a soldier through the lack of an allotment. He only knew of three boys from the village who had enlisted, and the families of every one of them had an allotment.

He pointed out that he had both dissenters and church people holding allotments in Winwick, and there were allotments freely available to those who wanted them. The holder of the largest allotment happened to be a man whose children attended the chapel Sunday school. He believed no one could say he had not done all in his power to assist the poor throughout his entire ministry.

He concluded his letter by saying: *Being by nature disposed to 'live peaceably with all men', I have refrained, as long as possible, from taking any notice of these false reports, feeling sure that they would never be believed by any who know me.*

It is remarkable to consider that two such strongly antagonistic factions could have existed within such a tiny community as Winwick. Mr Snitch alluded to the interesting fact that at one time, the chapel Sunday school had as many as seventy children on its books. By the date of this public spat, the number had apparently reduced to just nine.[xliii]

## You cannot always trust a policeman: PC Jacques, Huntingdon, 1870

Rather charmingly, the affair between Miss Mary Streather and her policeman beau, Mr Jacques, commenced by the latter writing to the lady at some time in 1868 to request her permission to 'keep company' with her, to which she had formally agreed.

Matters proceeded very satisfactorily and, in the words of the newspaper report, 'warm epistolary effusions' on the part of policeman ensued.

No doubt, when he was busy composing his warm epistles, he did not give any consideration to what they might like sound like when read out in open court by someone else. It must have been quite humiliating that, when this happened, it caused great laughter to roll around the court room.

In one of his letters to Miss Streather he said:

> *I went to bed at 5 o'clock this evening, and I was dreaming about you all the time. I had to make a cup of tea myself, but, my dear, it shall not be for long, for I intend you to do that...*

In case this was not recommendation enough, he wrote her another, saying:

> *You see, my dear, how I love – I love till my bones ache, and it is all for you ...*

Based on the letters, Miss Streather had no difficulty in persuading the jury (when they regained control of themselves) that there had been an engagement between them. Mr Jacques had married another lady, and so the case seemed rather clear cut.

There had been a suggestion of a quarrel between the parties. Miss Streather was asked to give evidence about it. It appeared to be concerned with her objection to Mr Jacques having been put on duty to help prevent a breach of the peace during the visit to the town of a Mr Murphy, presumably a Roman Catholic preacher. Not quite understanding the reason for her objection to his being on duty on such an occasion, the defence counsel asked her whether she was not, then, a staunch Protestant? To which the lady indignantly replied, 'Certainly not! I am Church of England!'

The jury liked her, and awarded her £20 compensation for the breach of promise, which, for someone in a modest station of life, was worth having.[xliv]

# Concealing, or not concealing? Elizabeth Pickering, Swineshead, 1861

The law provided that it was a crime for any woman who had given birth to a child, whether it was still alive at birth or not, to conceal the disposal of its body. The maximum sentence for this offence at this time was two years in prison. The law had been introduced to curb the clandestine disposal of illegitimate babies.

In 1861, Elizabeth Pickering, a single girl, had given birth to a baby girl alone and without help, in Swineshead. The baby was either stillborn or else she died more or less at birth.

She had not told anyone about the birth. What she did with the body of the child was to lay it in a water-filled ditch alongside a footpath, in the open. The following day, the body was discovered by her father, and the truth came out.

A surgeon examined the baby, and came to the conclusion that she may have breathed, but only faintly. Elizabeth was brought before the assizes on a charge of concealment of the birth, but the judge, after reviewing the law and applying it as he found it, had directed the jury to acquit her. Her actions had not amounted to concealment. [xlv]

# A short and unhappy life: Louisa Woodham, Stow Longa, 1870

This story highlights the miserable poverty of the poorest residents of our rural villages in the nineteenth century.

On 18 July 1870, Louisa Woodham was committed to the Huntingdon assizes charged with having murdered her infant child. She would have well known that she was would be sentenced to death by hanging if found guilty by the jury.

Louisa was unmarried, and was thirty years old, having been born and baptised in Stow in 1840. Despite being described as a spinster, Louisa seems long to have been the 'common law wife' of Samuel Mobbs of Stow, but for reasons best known to themselves, they did not marry until after these events.

Louisa was described as having given birth to many children before this date. The records are difficult to identify. Stow births were registered at St Neots. There are about a dozen births that could be attributed to her, including some recorded as simply 'male' or 'female' where a child was presumably stillborn. The only record that is incontrovertibly hers is that of the birth of 'Samuel Mobbs Woodham' who was of course Samuel Mobbs's son.

Louisa was said to be in the habit of spending her nights at her sister's house. Although it didn't specify which of her several sisters it was, it is most likely to have been Esther, a sister who was two years or so older than Louisa. The fact that Louisa had no home of her own at the age of thirty, despite having several dependent children, illustrates the precariousness of her position.

On 13 June that year, Louisa had given birth to a baby in the outside privy of her sister's house, alone and in secret. The child was either born dead, or died shortly after birth, of what cause is unknown. Bizarre as it might now sound, Louisa felt so unable to let it be known that she had given birth that she simply wrapped the baby up tightly in cloth and hid it in her sleeping room. It will come as no surprise that after a month had passed, others became aware of its presence.

The police were called, and Louisa was found at the public house in Stow where James Mobbs, Sam's brother, was innkeeper. She was questioned about the concealment of the birth of a child, and gave up to the police a key to a box that lay under her bed. The box was opened, and inside was found the body of the child, much decomposed, and wrapped in rags. Louisa was arrested on a charge of wilful murder, and appeared much affected, crying, and volubly admitting that she was completely to blame for what had happened.

A surgeon was called, and an autopsy was carried out on the baby. It was reported that it had been born at full term, and that there was evidence that it had breathed. The surgeon considered that it had died by violence.

The jury were directed by the judge that they needed to find two things in order to find a 'true bill' for murder: first, that Louisa's child had been born living, and second, that she had deliberately ended its life.

It must have come as a great relief to her, therefore, when the grand jury at the assizes found 'no true bill' for murder, but found instead a true bill for manslaughter and for concealment of a birth. The matter went forward to a trial, and the trial jury then acquitted her of manslaughter, but found her guilty of concealing the birth. She was sentenced to twelve months imprisonment with hard labour.

There is nothing to tell us what became of her other infants for the year in which she was incarcerated.

Louisa would have been due for release in July of 1871, but it seems that prison had not had the effect of reforming her.

On 25 November 1872, someone – later proved to have been Louisa – boldly walked into Mr and Mrs Carter's shoe shop in Kimbolton High Street. Without a blush, she announced that she had come on behalf of Mrs Bloodworth of Newtown, to fetch some boots for her. Mrs Bloodworth was the wife of Thomas Bloodworth, well-respected local landowner and farmer. She was a good customer of the Carters, and an order from her would have been attended to without question. Two pairs of boots of the requested size were duly produced and handed to Louisa and marked down to Mrs Bloodworth's account. This was repeated, and in all, four pairs of boots were handed over.

It was not long before the deception became apparent at the Bloodworth end of things. Two pairs of the boots were found by the local police sergeant to be in Louisa's possession, and her explanation was that she had bought one pair from a hawker, and another pair from Susannah Hall, the coalman's daughter. The other two pairs were found at an address at Twywell, but no explanation was given in the press reports as why the authorities thought it worth their while going there to look for them.

She was found guilty of obtaining goods by false pretences, and sentenced to three months imprisonment with hard labour. Her term of imprisonment commenced on 1 July 1872 and ended at the end of September. On 11 January 1873 she gave birth to Samuel, so she must have been in an interesting condition whilst carrying out her hard labour.

Prison was certainly not a deterrent for Louisa. At the Huntingdon petty sessions early in February 1873 she faced a charge of stealing linen, and her sister, Esther, was charged along with her. She turned up in court with the three-week-old baby Samuel in her arms. The two sisters were by this time living together in Catworth. Louisa was earning a living by 'mangling' laundry at Mrs Peacock's house, where washing was taken in from paying customers in the village. Unfortunately, some of what she mangled didn't make it back to the rightful owners. In particular, Mr Frederick Nicholson missed a sheet, a chemise, a child's nightshirt and a towel. He reported the loss, and the local constable – for some reason, we cannot imagine why – seems to have felt compelled to search Louisa's premises. He encountered a locked box, and may have feared what he would find in it, because it was he who had opened it three years before and found the dead body of her child inside. He requested the key from Louisa but she said she had lost it. He broke it open, and there he found the missing linen.

Esther was acquitted, as there was nothing to link her with the theft, but Louisa – whose only defence was that she had no idea how the items got into her box – was convicted.

This was not all, however. Whilst the constable had been searching their premises for the missing laundry items, he had noticed two sacks that he considered they had no business to have. They were being used as bedding, which gives some indication of the desperate poverty of these two women. The sacks carried the brand of the owner, James Watts, who identified them and valued them at 2s 6d the pair. The bench found both women guilty of having stolen them, and, noting her history, sentenced Louisa to three months in prison, and Esther to two months.

Both women had children depending upon them. Esther was a widow, with children aged twelve, ten, seven and three. Louisa was reported to have had several children, the youngest only three weeks old. How did they cope?

Louisa would have been released early in May 1873. Just under two years later, Samuel Mobbs finally made an honest woman of her, after which she seems to have kept clear of the courts and prison. The couple went on to have seven more children together over the ensuing nine years. Sam Mobbs seems to have had steady employment as an agricultural labourer and perhaps Louisa was not required to find anyone to trust her with their linen, their sacks or their boots. She lived on in Stow Longa till the age of eighty-five.

Perhaps because Stow was a small place, there were several intermarriages between the Mobbs family and the Woodhams. The two families came to public attention again in 1902 as a result of a terrible tragedy.

Clara Woodham of Stow had had an illegitimate child in 1895, whom she named Arthur Charles Woodham. He was known later as Arthur Charles Mobbs. She had afterwards married the assumed father, Tom Mobbs. When Arthur was eight years old, there had been a dreadful accident. His mother had left him just for a few minutes in the house, but when she returned, she had found him on the doorstep, still alive, but unable to speak. He died a few minutes later.

At the inquest on the little boy, an older boy, Benjamin Horsford Mash, said that whilst he was on his way to fetch milk from a neighbouring house he had spotted some sparrows on top of a haystack in a rickyard. He had gone back for his gun, and had shot a bird on some railings, and then one atop a barn. When he finally made it back to breakfast with his milk, to his horror there was Samuel Mobbs, informing his father that he had just shot the young lad. He went immediately to Arthur's house and saw the boy just before he expired. He had never considered that the bullets could travel so far as that.

On investigation, it was found that the bullet had travelled 114 yards. Benjamin would not have been able to see the doorway where poor Arthur was hit. The bullet had passed through a cloth that was pegged up to dry in an old plum tree in the garden, and had hit the lintel of the door, presumably ricocheting off, and into Arthur's lung and heart.

There was no prosecution, as a finding of accidental death was recorded. The effect on such a tight and interlinked community of an event such as this must have been shattering, and particularly on Benjamin, who had to live with the knowledge that he had taken the life of Clara's young son.

For those who are familiar with the so-called 'St Neots Poisoning Case' referred to in the introduction, Benjamin's name will be familiar as the cousin of the victim in that tragedy.

## Hospitality to die for: Thomas Mawby of the Crown Inn, Stilton, 1737

Stilton was a place through which many people passed in days gone by, situated, as it was, on the old North Road, and served by many inns and visited regularly by the stagecoaches. People came and went, and there may be some who came intending to leave, but did not quite make it out for one reason or another. Perhaps because they were brutally taken advantage of, and not missed, for example.

This is a story of a murder that went unpunished.

Unfortunately, we can never know the identity of the fellow whose life was taken, but he was supposed to have been from Scotland, and to have been quite a poor man. He was described as a pedlar.

It was said that he had come to Stilton in 1737 to ply his trade there, presumably because of the opportunities presented by crowds of transient people.

Mr Mawby and his wife kept the Crown Inn at Stilton. A man named James Capes said that he was 'on the ramble' towards midnight one night, when he saw the gates at the entrance of the Crown open, and decided to go and chance his luck at getting himself a mug of ale. He knocked at the kitchen door, and Mrs Mawby called out to see who was there. Hearing who it was, she told him she was not drawing any ale, and that was that.

Capes was a nosy man, and observing that there was a light on in the kitchen, applied his organ of vision to the keyhole. What he says he saw was definitely not intended to be seen by anyone other than the occupants of that kitchen.

He said that Mrs Mawby and her ostler, Perkins, were busy stripping the clothes from the body of a man lying dead on the kitchen table. He overheard Perkins say, 'I'll have his shirt!' and Mrs Mawby replying, 'So you shall! And anything else.' Mr Mawby then said, 'See what a little knock will do for a man in liquor!' making the evening's sport now apparently perfectly clear.

The next thing he said he heard was Mrs Mawby asking, 'Where shall we bury him?' Discussion ensued, and it was decided to put the body into the ground under 'the six stalls window', presumably referring to an area close to the stables. Mrs Mawby said they should cover him up, and the dung would ensure he stayed out of sight.[xlvi]

This evidence was given to the police by Mr Capes some eighteen years after the events he was describing. So, why did Mr Capes not come forward sooner?

When this question was put to him, he said he had been loath to 'take away so many lives' – those of the innkeeper, his wife and the ostler. He had kept it to himself for all those years, but now he had gone through a serious bout of illness the previous winter, and one night when he had been unable to find sleep, he had thought he heard a voice, saying 'Declare! Declare! Declare!' He had pulled the bed curtains back to see who was there, but there was no one to be seen, and it had left him uneasy ever since. After so many years, there was now only Mr Mawby left alive, his wife and the ostler having predeceased him.

Great interest was aroused by the curious facts of the case. On 13 May 1755 the Rt. Hon. Lord Carysfort, the Rev. Dr Neve and John Wildboar (all magistrates) assembled at Stilton to conduct an investigation into the evidence. At the end of it, the place near to the stables was excavated, and a body was indeed discovered where Capes had said it would be. Thomas Mawby was committed for trial at Huntingdon assizes, charged with murder.

And frustratingly, dear reader, here the trail runs cold.

Was this all a concocted tale to get the good innkeeper into the direst trouble imaginable? Was there a personal grudge at the bottom of it? Or was the story a true one, but it was just so long after the events that there was no reliable evidence to bring anyone to trial? Or had Capes committed the murder himself?

The only sure thing is that Thomas Mawby remained firmly on this side of the veil until about 1765, when his will was proved by a cousin. The provisions he made on his death were very tenderly recorded, and recognised the family of his first wife as well as his second wife, but principally made arrangements for the support and education of his daughter (and only child) by his first wife. It is clear from the terms of his will that he was very close to his parents and that he recognised family ties with aunts and cousins as being important to him. Whether such a man could have dispatched a customer and made such a poor job of disposing of the body is a very interesting question.

## When it pays to look like your father: the strange case of Day-v-Day; Wornditch, 1822

This is an extraordinary case of alleged imposture with the intent to take an inheritance. Wornditch, at the date of these proceedings, was a hamlet adjacent to Kimbolton, and consisted of the 'great house', Wornditch Hall, and a collection of farms and labourers' dwellings. Today there is little left to suggest such a distinct community existed.

The Day family were a genteel old local family, of some considerable means, whose seat, from the early eighteenth century onwards, was at the Hall.

In order to understand the significance of the allegations made in this family dispute, it is necessary to understand the provisions of the will of 'old' Mr Thomas Day, who died in 1775. He had left his estates in Wornditch and Spaldwick to his elder son, Thomas, but subject to a condition that it would pass back to his younger son, John, if Thomas had no male heir.

Thomas, who had looked as if he was going to remain a bachelor all his life, had married late in life, no doubt to the frustration of his brother, John. His wife conveniently bore him one son, also called Thomas. It therefore appeared

28 *Wornditch Hall.*

that John was now out of the frame so far as his father's will was concerned. Or, was he?

John was not quite satisfied about this nephew. There were some odd circumstances that made him think that Mrs Day was pulling a fast one.

A lawsuit was commenced in 1784 in which the paternity of Thomas the youngest was contested.

Essentially, the allegation was that Mrs Day, in view of her husband's great need of an heir, had appropriated someone else's baby and had pretended to the world at large (and also to Mr Day) that it was Mr Day's child.

In November of 1774, Mrs Day had taken herself off to Leigh, near Keele, where her parents (Mr and Mrs Lakin) lived. She told people there that she was expecting a child.

John Day managed to produce several witnesses who were neighbours of Mr and Mrs Lakin, and who saw plenty of Mrs Day whilst she was there. These ladies said that Mrs Day bore no appearance of being in the condition she claimed to be. A servant to the Lakin household gave evidence that after staying at the house for three months, Mrs Day and her mother left without any baby in their possession.

Another servant, to Mrs Day's uncle in Leigh, said that when Mrs Day visited their household, she actually shared a bed with Mrs Day and took care of her laundry, and there was no sign that she was expecting.

Six witnesses also gave evidence that Mrs Day had been extremely anxious to take possession of the illegitimate child of her own brother, and had wanted to take him away with her back to Huntingdon. The mother of the baby had at first agreed and had given the little boy over to her, but then repented of her decision and asked for the baby back. Mrs Day had refused to give him back, and the woman had gone to a magistrate and obtained an order that he be returned to her.

In the meantime, Mrs Day had clothed the child using baby clothes that she had brought with her from Huntingdon. When she was obliged to give him back to his mother, she had stripped him of all the clothes, saying that if she had to give up the baby, she would keep the clothes. The evidence for this having occurred was given by very credible witnesses, including the parish overseer of the poor, who had been present in the magistrate's house when it had happened.

The son of an innkeeper at Lichfield testified that Mrs Day and her mother had stayed at the inn, but had had no baby with them. The innkeeper's mother had asked Mrs Day if she had any family, and Mrs Day had said she had no living child, but had had a daughter, who had died. Only a short time after this, Mrs Day had turned up at the house of another aunt, Mrs Harris, who lived at Atherstone, carrying a baby which she said was hers. Her aunt was astonished: she could not understand why she had not heard that her niece was expecting. Mrs Day told her that she had been to her mother's house for her 'lying-in' and that the baby was now five weeks old.

From the house of this aunt, Mrs Day went by stagecoach in the direction of Leicester, and arrived at the White Hart Inn, in Kettering, where she was known to the innkeeper. He gave evidence that she had the baby with her then, and from his inn she took a chaise to Kimbolton. The journey was complete, and Mrs Day was now at home, with a son.

Intimate friends of Mr Day gave evidence in court that Mr Day had often voiced suspicions to them that the boy was neither his nor his wife's: he did not believe that his wife had been expecting a baby when she had left Kimbolton to go to Leigh. He never had the little boy christened. Very sadly, evidence was also given that Mrs Day had no affection for the child, and was very unkind to him – in fact, not at all like a mother towards him. She was so unkind to the baby that Mr Day had sent it away to Biggleswade to be

29 *View of Kimbolton High Street.*

wet-nursed, and the nurse kept him upwards of a year. All of this does suggest a lack of parental acceptance, and it must have seemed very odd indeed to their acquaintances.

A few years later, it seems Mrs Day left her husband and went back to live with her parents in Staffordshire. There was much evidence given that she was mentally deranged. Mr Day confided to an acquaintance that she had been in a 'lowly' position in society when he had married her, but that she had been a very bad wife. She had pilfered from him, she had tried to burn the house down, and had jumped out of a window shouting 'Murder!' in order to vex him. Information about the baby gradually came out, and Mr Day said to an acquaintance that he would go to Staffordshire and try to find out the truth, but that he would never abandon the child, who depended on him. From this, it would seem that he was more of a father to the child than Mrs Day was a mother.

So, what exactly had gone on in the time between Mrs Day leaving Leigh (with no sign of a child) and her arrival at her aunt's house in Atherstone with a baby in her arms?

In Mrs Day's favour, several female servants of the Kimbolton household were called who testified that they had known that she was expecting a baby before she had set off to her parents' house, and some said they had helped her to pack 'child-bed' clothes into her luggage to take with her. Her physician from Kimbolton also confirmed that he had believed her to be pregnant before she left home to go to Leigh.

One witness, Mrs Rutter, testified that she had met with Mrs Day in Staffordshire and had accompanied her to her father's house where she had stayed with her for a month until she was delivered of her baby, a boy. Only she and the midwife had been present at the birth.

Many witnesses from Kimbolton and the local area commented on how much the baby, and later the boy, resembled Mr Day.

Mrs Day admitted at one point that she had told her husband that the child was not his, but only because she had parted from him and wished him to give the child up to her, which he perhaps would have done if he had understood it to be an imposter. Of course, he did not do so.

John Day had a difficult task. As the judge put it, since he wished to assert that his brother was not the true father of the little boy, he must either produce the boy's true father or else leave him with the one he currently had.

The court found against John, and confirmed Thomas to be the true son of Mr Thomas Day senior.

Then, a short time after the trial, Mrs Rutter and her mother went to see a magistrate in Staffordshire and confessed that they had perjured themselves: they had not been present at the birth of any baby to Mrs Day, and their consciences now pricked them (and Mrs Day had failed to pay them their promised reward for testifying in her favour).

They also said that another woman, named Harris, had been taken by Mrs Day to the court hearing, but that she had refused to testify in her favour, threatening Mrs Day that if she was given the witness stand, she would make sure everyone knew where the baby had really come from. Consequently, Mrs Day had taken care to lock her into a room at the Crown Inn at Huntingdon until the trial was over. Mrs Harris had the whole story, it was said.

Unfortunately, John Day was not in a position to finance any more litigation, his purse having taken a huge hit in 1784. He died in 1795, and his own son – another John – continued the battle. Mrs Day had also, by this time, died.

Counsel for John Day Jnr laid out before the jury the full details of Mrs Day's various transactions in Staffordshire after she had left Kimbolton at the end of 1774. It involved numerous attempts to secure a baby from several different women, all meeting with failure for one reason or another, until in the company of Mrs Harris she had been introduced to Ann Osborne, from Birmingham Workhouse, who had given birth a few weeks before. She, at last, was willing to hand over her baby.

Other witnesses gave evidence that at the date when Mrs Day should have been busy giving birth (if her story was true), she was, in fact, attending the baptism of a young cousin to whom she stood as godmother, and gave no appearance of being either pregnant or of having just given birth. The baptismal records were produced to prove it.

Witnesses were called to confirm that the boy bore a strong resemblance to his alleged natural mother, Ann Osborne. Still others were called who said that Mr Day had been a man of very 'singular' appearance, and that young Thomas resembled him strongly.

The judge informed the jury that evidence of resemblance to a parent was not sufficient evidence on its own, but that it could corroborate other evidence, and be persuasive. He said that one of the strongest pieces of evidence in favour of young Thomas was that Mr Day had accepted him as his son, by leaving him his property in his will on that basis. There could be no greater signal of paternal acknowledgement.

After many hours of hearing evidence, the jury deliberated for just an hour and a half before deciding, once again, in favour of young Thomas.

It was said of the young man that he was in every way a perfect gentleman, and that he was a credit to his father in every respect.[xlvii]

Sometime after the conclusion of the second case, Thomas voluntarily entered into a settlement of the lands at Wornditch in favour of his cousin, John, and retained just his late father's property at Spaldwick for himself. This seems to have brought the dispute finally to an end.

## Words from the grave: John Chapman, Huntingdon, 16 August 1787

John Chapman was convicted of stealing twenty-four sheep from a Mr Prime, of Orwell, near Cambridge. He was sentenced to death, and was hanged at Mill Common in Huntingdon on 17 August 1787. The day before his sentence was carried out, John wrote to what the press rather ungenerously called the woman who 'passed for his wife':

*Dear Girl,*

*This letter is the last you will ever have from me, as tomorrow morning I must die (and most justly) tor the offence I have committed against the laws of God and my country. The time is now approaching when I must give a solemn account to that Judge of Judges, how I have spent this life, excuses with Him will avail nothing; all I can say is, Lord be merciful to me, a sinner! The most principal charge I have to give you is respecting my boy; instruct him in the paths of religion and virtue; teach him the excellencies of industry, and the evils that accrue from idleness, that great source of all the villainy which has brought thousands to that ignominious death I am going to suffer. God forbid that he, or anyone should die the wretched death I must: but take warning by me, and shun the paths of wickedness, that they may attain the heavenly promise made them in scripture, 'a crown of righteousness'. Shed not a tear on my account, for such worthless wretch deserves no pity. JOHN CHAPMAN*

## The value of money: James Watkins, Huntingdon Races, 20 July 1870

Here is an example of enterprise that involved taking advantage of a really gullible punter at the races in the summer of 1870. It is unlikely to have been the first (or last) time that Mr Watkins practised this little trick, but it was not without its risks.

Henry Sales of Stukeley was enjoying a day out at the races in Brampton on 20 July when he spotted Mr Watkins, standing on a stool near to the grandstand. In his hand, Mr Watkins was holding a piece of paper, and in the paper lay two half-crowns, two shilling pieces and a thimble. He was calling out, 'Who will give me a shilling for this?'

It is human nature to want to believe in an offer like this, but equally it ought to be apparent to anyone with any intelligence (especially at the races!) that this bargain was never going to turn out well for the punter. Watkins approached Mr Sales and asked him to go for it, but he did not do so at that stage. Watkins continued to call out, and upped the stakes by adding 'If you think my money is good, here is another shilling!' and he lay another shilling coin onto the piece of paper. He went on 'I can't afford to sell all like this, but if I sell this one, I guarantee to sell six more in five minutes!'

This was too much for Henry Sales, he fell for it and purchased the paper for a shilling. Now, we all know, don't we, what the result of this was going to be? Why didn't Henry know?

He opened up the paper, and found that he had two ha'pennies, two farthings and, of course, the thimble.

These facts were laid before the jury at the assizes who found Watkins guilty of obtaining money under false pretences. He was sentenced to two months imprisonment with hard labour.[xlviii]

Henry Sales sadly lost his young wife in 1875, and seems to have struggled on the domestic front: in 1879 he was prosecuted for failing to provide his children with a proper education and was ordered to ensure that they all attend school. If not schooled, hopefully at least a little more 'street-wise' than papa.

## When all else fails, just deny everything: Mr Crick of Houghton, 1888

Mr Crick was a curmudgeonly old rat-catcher from Houghton, who had ordered coal from Boltons, coal merchants in St Ives, but had not got round to paying for it. Eventually, the Boltons took him to court for their money.

The dialogue as reported in the Cambridge Independent Press proceeded as follows:

His Honour the Judge: *Then you sold the coals to this rat-catcher?*

Plaintiff: *Yes, your Honour, in the years 1886 and 1887. I sent round carts until the end of March 1887. My wife and I went round afterwards, and we took the defendant his bill. I claimed then for more than I now claim, but the defendant said he did not owe for more than one ton. He said that my son had told him [...] he could have them at lower price. I then agreed to take 16s. for the ton [...] He said he would pay in a short time.*

Defendant (in a loud voice): *I never had a bit of coal of him in my life!*

His Honour (to the plaintiff): *Are you quite sure that this is the man?*

Plaintiff: *I am quite sure.*

Mrs Bolton was called, and said she made out the books. She personally saw the bill being handed to the defendant.

Defendant (loudly): *I have never seen the lady before in my life!*

The plaintiff's son was then called, and said he was present when his mother saw the defendant in the front of his house at Houghton, and the defendant had promised to pay in a week or two's time.

Defendant (loudly): *I have never seen the gentleman before in my life! I have never had a bit of coal of Mr Bolton in my life! It is false if they say so. Bolton did not come to me, nor his wife, nor his son!*

His Honour: *Is there any other person of your name in the village?*

Defendant: *No, sir.*

His Honour: *Judgment for the plaintiff, with costs.*

Defendant: *I am not prepared to pay!*

His Honour: *I am prepared make you pay … Can you pay a shilling a month? What are the profits of rat-catching?*

Defendant: *None at all! I don't get anything!*

His Honour: *Then how do you live?*

Defendant: *As well as I can.*

His Honour: *You seem to do well upon it. I order you to pay 4s per month.*

## Little witches: Huntingdon, 1827

This is a very shocking case, and doubtless it would have received considerable publicity locally at the time. However, the only report of it that can now be found occurs in the Berkshire Chronicle, giving some indication of the notoriety of the events.

Three little girls, Ann Skinner aged ten, Mary Bosworth aged nine and Mary Mall aged eight were all put on trial at the Huntingdon assizes in March 1827 charged with having murdered Sarah Bright, a little girl who was not quite four years old.

They had apparently fixed pins into the end of sticks, and had thrust them into her body.

They were all acquitted, on the basis of their age.[xlix]

## Improving the quality

At a sitting of the Huntingdon assizes in 1619, the sheriff of the county had been reproved by the judge (Sir John Doddridge) for the poor quality of the individuals he had selected for the grand jury. His lordship felt that the men in question were not sufficiently representative of the elite of the town.

On the occasion of the next sitting of the court, the sheriff took no chances. He made a very careful selection, and this is the list of the persons put forward to the judge:

| | |
|---|---|
| Maximilian King of Toseland | Robert Yeoman of Barham |
| Henry Prince of Godmanchester | Stephen Pope of Old Weston |
| George Duke of Somersham | Humphrey Cardinal of Kimbolton |
| Edward Earl of Hartford | William Bishop of Buckden |
| Robert Lord of Waresley | John Abbot of Stukeley |
| Richard Baron of Bythorn | John Archdeacon of Paxton |
| Robert Baron of Winwick | Richard Friar of Ellington |
| Edward Knight of St Neots | Henry Monk of Stukeley |
| Peter Esquire of Easton | Edward Priest of Grafham and |
| George Gentleman of Spaldwick | Richard Deacon of Catworth. |

His lordship applauded the sheriff's hard work, and the sitting commenced.[l]

30 *Tomb Effigy of Sir John Doddridge. Judge Doddridge was known as 'the sleeping judge', because of his habit of closing his eyes when hearing legal arguments in court.*

## Killing by kindness: James Inglett, Houghton, 1841

This is the sad story of an elderly man who tried to help a young woman in his village, but through ineptitude, mistake or other innocent reason, he actually caused her death.

James Inglett was a farmer. He was ninety-four at the date of these events, and had practised as what was termed a 'cow leech' for most of his life, in and around Houghton. A cow-leech was an untrained veterinary attendant who treated sick animals (and, it seems, occasionally humans) using country remedies.

It was said that his great venerability and experience in the so-called healing arts meant that he was held in great esteem by his poorer neighbours, and he had enjoyed an unsullied reputation up to this point in his life.

A young lady from the village named Elizabeth Harlott had suffered a lot of ill-health during the previous year, and had exhausted all the remedies that the apothecary could supply, without getting any better. At about Christmas time in 1840, James had been sent for, and he had administered a dose of a medicine that had initially made her very sick, but as a result of which she had then seemed to be rather better.

James called to see her again on 11 January, and left her another dose of the same medicament, which she took a little later in the day. After taking it, she was sick and in excruciating pain, and her condition worsened steadily into the night. She suffered from an intolerable thirst, and the pain was unbearable. She died the next morning.

The usual offices followed, with a village burial, and no doubt her family thought that life must move on. However, her death was followed by a week or two of intense speculation which reached the coroner, and he ordered that her body should be exhumed and an inquest be held.

The autopsy revealed severe inflammation of her stomach, but otherwise no disease, and the inquest jury therefore decided that whatever James had given her had caused the inflammation that had led to her death. As a result, he was indicted for murder, and immediately taken to Huntingdon gaol to await his trial. It must have been a bewildering translation from aged country cow-leech to defendant in a murder case.

James said to Elizabeth's family that he had given her only half a grain of arsenic in the mixture, and it could not have hurt her because he had given his own son and others double that amount, and more, without any ill effects. At the trial, evidence was given that he had told Elizabeth's sister that he wouldn't have given her the medicine at all if he had known that her stomach was not strong enough to take it, as he never intended to do her any harm. The woman spoke very kindly of his careful attention to her sister.

There does not seem to have been any appetite during the trial to prove that James had any deliberate intention to kill Elizabeth, so the matter came down to whether or not he had committed manslaughter. The judge told the jury that if they found that Elizabeth's death was the result of the medicine James had administered, they must then decide whether James had exercised a lack of proper caution in giving it to her. If so, he would be guilty of manslaughter. The jury took a long time to reach a decision, but they found him guilty.

The judge said that it was in the public interest to make it known that those who administer poisons to others, who die as a consequence, will be guilty of manslaughter. However, he was at pains not to inflict a harsh punishment on James, who had already been in prison on remand for six weeks. He sentenced him to a further fourteen days. It was said that James's silvery hair, respectful manner and 'mild countenance' thoroughly recommended him to everyone present in court. He survived his incarceration by about three years, and must have just reached the age of a hundred by the date of his death in 1844. He may well have been the oldest prisoner to be incarcerated at Huntingdon gaol.

# Defeating the humane intentions of government: Norman Cross, 1801

The presence on the margins of our county of some 7,000 Napoleonic prisoners of war between 1797 and 1814 caused some civic challenges. The prisoners themselves at Norman Cross occasionally committed crimes and required trial and punishment, and sometimes their mere existence was the cause of new and inventive misdemeanours on the part of the local residents.

The prisoners were permitted to earn a living by selling whatever they could make from the materials available to them, and this resulted in some outstandingly beautiful handicrafts created from bone, wood, straw and other materials that were readily to hand. However, they were, understandably, subject to a specific prohibition against using anything that belonged to the prison itself. There were notices posted throughout the area, warning the public not to purchase government property from the prisoners. The temptation, unfortunately, was sometimes just too great.

In January of 1801, a relatively well-to-do resident of Yaxley, named Jeremiah Askew, was found to have been colluding with the prisoners in the illegal trade of their clothing and straw mattresses, amongst other items, and to have been doing it for some long time, and in great quantities.[li] Even in those days, government property was clearly marked with an arrow, so that there could be no mistaking it, even if you couldn't read the notices.

Jeremiah, who was described as 'an opulent tradesman' and who was a baker and miller, was brought before the Huntingdon assizes, where he was

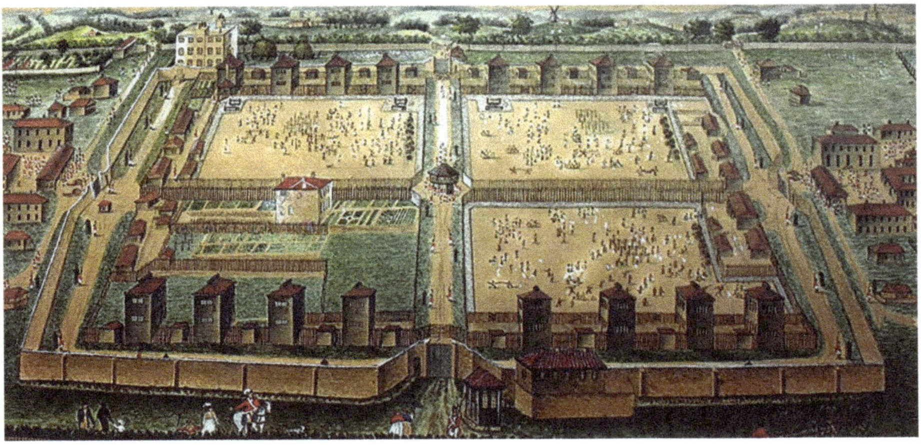

31 *Norman Cross prison camp.*

convicted and ordered to be placed in the pillory for an hour and then to be imprisoned for two years.[lii]

The pillory in Yaxley had been instituted in the late thirteenth century, and had been used more or less continually to allow members of the public to express their disapproval of offenders. Its use, however, gradually declined in the decades following Jeremiah's sentence, as it became increasingly clear that the effect of it was to place control of punishment in the hands of the public (or the mob), instead of the state.

There were some fairly gruesome (and even fatal) outcomes to a stint in the pillory that rendered the nature and extent of an offender's punishment sometimes both unpredictable and grossly disproportionate.

It was reported that whilst Jeremiah's dishonesty and profiteering were bad enough, the worst aspect of his behaviour was that he knowingly left the prisoners without their clothes and bedding in the depths of winter 'and thereby defeating the humane intentions of government'.[liii]

32 *The public enjoying a day out at the pillory.*[liv]

It seems fair to conclude that Jeremiah was something of a scapegoat. Following his conviction, the government took the opportunity of drawing maximum attention to his punishment by posting notices in newspapers right across the country as a warning to others.

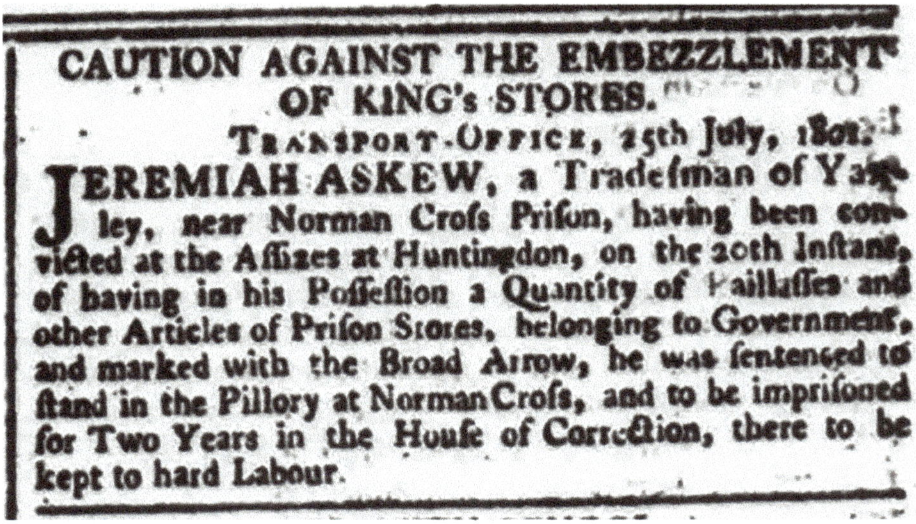

CAUTION AGAINST THE EMBEZZLEMENT OF KING's STORES.

TRANSPORT-OFFICE, 25th July, 1801.

JEREMIAH ASKEW, a Tradesman of Yaxley, near Norman Cross Prison, having been convicted at the Assizes at Huntingdon, on the 20th Instant, of having in his Possession a Quantity of Paillasses and other Articles of Prison Stores, belonging to Government, and marked with the Broad Arrow, he was sentenced to stand in the Pillory at Norman Cross, and to be imprisoned for Two Years in the House of Correction, there to be kept to hard Labour.

33

He seems to have survived the experience. He returned to Yaxley, where he lived until his death at the age of 87.

## A free holiday at The George Hotel: Gustave Henry Grace, Huntingdon, December 1880

This gentleman's name was not, in fact, Gustave Henry Grace, but William Ely Ainge. However, he used the surname Grace for the purpose of his sojourn in Huntingdon, and it was as Gustave Henry Grace that he was tried and convicted of obtaining goods and services under false pretences. The only record of a person of that name is the criminal record that resulted from his luxury spree at the George Hotel, in Huntingdon.

Mr Ainge appears to have come to Huntingdon for the sole purpose of a

34 *The George Hotel, Huntingdon.*

free slap-up holiday, and managed to get a jolly good one for the best part of three months. He did not, however, bring any luggage with him, which in those days was often regarded with suspicion. He explained it away at the hotel by telling them that his belongings had been sent to the Fountain Inn by mistake, and this seems to have been accepted. There is no evidence that it ever turned up, however.

The landlord of the George Hotel, Mr Goodliff, felt confident that he had a guest of good social and professional standing, and as a result was content to allow him credit at the hotel, and even had him to dine with his family.

His confidence arose from Mr Ainge's having asserted that he was a junior partner in the law firm of Barrell, Rodway & Barrell of Liverpool, enjoying a very good income and with the prospect of earning even more in a year or two. He said that he had come to Huntingdon with a large advance of cash from his firm, for the express purpose of investing in mortgages in the Huntingdon area. On the strength of this story, Mr Goodliff let him have the run of the hotel, and observed him consume the best of everything that was on offer – 'on tick' of course.

Mr Ainge had a black briefcase with him, and left the hotel every day (after a splendid breakfast) giving every appearance of heading off to transact some business. He also enjoyed a considerable amount of hunting and what was termed 'other expensive amusements'.

To take part in hunting as a hotel guest meant hiring a steed, and Mr Goodliff was good enough to supply his needs on five or six occasions, not just the horse but also the breeches, the boots and the whip. Hiring a horse for hunting was notoriously expensive, quite apart from those other unknown expensive amusements. He must, presumably, have had some ready cash about him, as no mention was made in the reports of any other victims of his deceit.

On 3 December, Mr Goodliff applied to his guest for a payment towards his ever-increasing hotel tab. This was when it became clear that Gustave was not really Gustave, and that he definitely was not a partner in a law firm.

There really was a law firm in Liverpool called Barrell, Rodway & Barrell, but the senior partner of the firm later confirmed in court that 'Gustave' was not a partner and that, in fact, he had never seen the man before.

The hotel bill exceeded £51 by the time it dawned on Mr Goodliff that 'Gustave' had moved in for good unless he did something about it, and so he called in the police, who searched his room. There they found a bible containing an inscription with his real name – William Ely Ainge – on the fly leaf. Articles of his clothing bore the same name.

William was arrested and appeared before the magistrates on 14 December, when he was committed for trial at the quarter sessions on a charge of deception. He made no reply to the charge against him, and did not wish to question any of the witnesses.

At his trial, William was described as a property broker, which was an occupation approximately akin to an estate agent. He was charged with obtaining board and lodging by false pretences, with intent to defraud. He pleaded not guilty, not on the basis that he denied the basic facts, but on the basis that he had not intended to be dishonest.[lv]

In his defence, his solicitor said that William had not come to Huntingdon with the purpose of taking advantage of Mr Goodliff's good nature as a host, but, having come to the hotel, he got himself into the position of not being able to settle the bill. That placed him in a dilemma, because if he ran away it would be dishonest, whereas to remain (and enjoy the liberal table and other benefits on offer) gave him a chance to try to work out how he could raise the money to pay what he owed. That was in fact the very opposite of 'dishonest'. His solicitor said that it was, at worst, a case of mere civil debt.

He put into evidence a most desperate letter written by William to Mr

Goodliff on the day before the trial, imploring him to drop the charges and allow him to find a way to pay the bill. This is an extract from the letter, the original of which repeated the same sentiments many times over, and which was read out to the jury:

> *Dear Sir*
>
> *In the event of my urgent endeavours to obtain the money wherewith to effect a settlement with you not being in time for tomorrow, I beg to implore your forgiveness for mercy for the deception I have practised upon you during the last two months or so. Firstly, on account of my poor wife and six little children, who are entirely dependent upon me for their support. Secondly, I am sure, from your natural kindness and disposition, you would hesitate to blast the future of any young man's career, and that will undoubtedly be the result should you succeed in obtaining a conviction against me. Not only so, the stigma would attach itself to the poor innocent little children of which I am the unhappy father. I know I have acted very wrong – wickedly: but if you could only see your way to forgive me, you would be doing a mercy, not to me, but to the poor little girls and boys who are not able to keep themselves ...*

He said that the whole purpose of his visit to Huntingdon had been to see if his grandfather, a Mr French, who farmed over 300 acres at Hilton near Huntingdon, could spare him a few hundred pounds, but his grandfather had not been susceptible to being tapped, because the farm was making a frightful loss.

William's connection to Mr French (who certainly existed) is not borne out by the available records, but one would hope that he would know who his grandparents were.

He signed the letter:

> *Again asking your kind indulgence and mercy tomorrow for which I shall be grateful till my dying day I am respectfully yours,*
> *GHG*
> *Pray excuse the hurriedly-written letter: once more asking for your mercy, for the sake of my children.*

35 *The Ainge family home in Craven Terrace, Halifax.*

It is interesting indeed that he was still sticking to the initials 'GHG' despite having been 'outed' as William Ainge.

It was perfectly true that William had a wife and six children, but his wife certainly considered herself to be Mrs Ainge, not Mrs Grace, and the six 'poor innocent little children' all thought of themselves as little Ainges.

The couple had been living in a rented house in Craven Terrace in Halifax, which would have been a tight squeeze for such a large family. William had been employed in other capacities than property broker (including as a warehouseman) suggesting that his career and prospects were perhaps not very stable even before these events. Just before his 'spree' at Huntingdon they had relocated to Birkenhead, where he began to refer to himself as an 'accountant'. He seems to have entered an accountancy partnership there called 'Walter, Craven & Ainge', whose business was certainly connected to property broking. At the date of this little bit of trouble, his children were aged between one and eight years old.

The jury listened to the rambling and plaintive letter, and this closed the case for William's defence. They retired to consider their verdict, and took only a few minutes to decide that he was guilty.

When passing sentence, the chairman of the quarter sessions told him that his conduct had been 'particularly atrocious' and that he had exhibited 'gross cruelty' – by which he may have meant to his wife and family, rather than to Mr Goodliff, since he also said that if he had been in Mr Goodliff's position he would have taken a little more care before dispensing his hospitality so freely. He went rather to town in his address, telling William that he was convicted of a gross offence that sapped at the very foundations of society, and sentenced him to two years in prison with hard labour.

That was quite a tough sentence. He would have been in prison until the end of 1882 (and would certainly have worked off all his free breakfasts).

The sentence caused some astonishment in certain quarters. The chairman of the quarter sessions had said, when delivering the sentence, that the reason for a stiff punishment was in part some other conduct of Mr Grace's that had come to his attention and which he found objectionable. This, of course, was not his duty: no evidence had been brought in about this other matter; William had had no chance to refute it or question any witnesses, and it was therefore utterly subjective. It was referred to later as 'convicting a man of one offence and punishing him for another, and another which was unsupported by a tittle of evidence.'

Apparently, his wife, Susan, stuck by him. When he came out of prison, they took the understandable decision to get as far away from his past as they could, by leaving the country. William took his family to Canada in 1883, and practised as an accountant there for a few years before moving to New York. Three more children gladdened the Ainge hearth. The information he proffered for the USA census does not quite accord with this timetable of events, but it would be churlish to suppose that this was because William wished to conceal anything from them whilst practising there as a public accountant and auditor.

36 *The Fountain Inn, Huntingdon.*

He does seem genuinely to have achieved a fresh start to his life in America. In a volume entitled *The History of Chautauqua County and its People* published in 1921, William had an entry all to himself. [lvi] In it, he professed to be the (illegitimate) son of a farmer of 800 acres in Warwickshire (whose identity, however, cannot be verified from the available records). The article records that William was president of the W. Ely Ainge Accounting Company of Ohio and Pennsylvania, and that his company employed 'a considerable force of highly trained specialists'. It seems that he had put the George Hotel, Mr Goodliff and Huntingdon gaol behind him, and made a success of his life, but there can be hardly any doubt that in the process he had concealed a past that would have been a bar to such a career.

William died in New York in 1929.

As a post-script to William's story, it is notable that his son, Percy, born in Canada in 1885, does not seem to have inherited his father's high standards as a tender husband and father: having married in the USA, he was sued by his wife for kicking, cursing, abusing and beating her, on which basis she divorced him.

## Snapshot of quarter sessions cases for January 1869

The court was not troubled with any major crimes at this session, but it is striking, and thought-provoking, to see how often prosecutions were brought for the theft of clothing:

*Susan Clark*, stealing clothing the property of Robert Margetts, Esq., Huntingdon.

*Susan Clark*, stealing tablecloths, sheets, etc., the property of S. E. Cooch Esq., Huntingdon.

*Luke Knight*, stealing wheat, the property Wm. Mason Cave, at Stilton.

*Henry Oakes*, stealing a pair of trousers, the property Bennett Sharp, Buckden.

*William Turner*, stealing a pair of trousers, the property of Bennett Sharp, Buckden.

*Oliver Thorpe*, stealing two mops, the property of Wm. Cliffe and Wm. Carter, St Neots.

*John Cambridge*, stealing £3, the property of Robert Squires, Wistow.

*James Buck*, stealing a great coat, etc., the property of Henry Cope, Sawtry.

*Mary A. Fountain*, receiving a great coat, etc, the property of Henry Cope, Sawtry.

*George Hailes*, stealing silver spoons, etc., belonging to Rev. John Bell, at Brington.

*George Hailes*, stealing flower seeds, etc., the property of John Ingram, Huntingdon.

*George Hailes*, stealing clothing etc., belonging to Henry Smith, of Great Catworth.

37 *Catworth, around 1900.*

## Not all rabbits are equal: Kimbolton, June 1842

The following sentences were imposed at the summer quarter sessions in Huntingdon in 1842:

*Samuel Mason,* convicted of having trespassed on the Duke of Manchester's land at Kimbolton, in search of conies: fine £.3. 6s. 6d.

*Matthew Mason,* convicted of having trespassed on the Duke of Manchester's land at Kimbolton, in search of conies: fine £3 6s. 6d.

*George King,* convicted of having trespassed on the land of Samuel Newton, Esq., at Yelling, in search of conies: fine £2. 9s. 6d. [lvii]

## Proof that a good counsel is worth his weight in linen: Susannah Clark, Huntingdon, 1869

Samuel Cooch was a very well-known and respected coal and timber merchant. He was also an alderman of Huntingdon, a magistrate, and held the office of 'Distributor of Stamps' (i.e. stamps for the discharge of government stamp duties). His residence was opposite All Saints Church by the market square in Huntingdon, and he kept a small staff of servants: usually just a cook, a housekeeper and a housemaid.

Robert Margetts was an equally illustrious businessman within the borough. He was a wine merchant, maltster and miller.

Susannah Clark went to work as a maid in the Cooch household, Mr Cooch having taken care to receive a decent reference for her before he allowed her to be taken on. Her reference had come from the Hon. Mrs Neville, wife of the Hon. Latimer Neville, later 6th Baron Braybrooke, who had a residence in Chesterton Lane in Cambridge. Whether you consider that the honourable lady was mistaken in her view of the character of her former servant depends on how you view the evidence given at Susannah's trial.

Susannah was a blacksmith's daughter, born in Cawston, near Norwich, the third of fifteen children. Perhaps this, and the concomitant scarcity of personal possessions and personal space, made her enterprising and resourceful.

For reasons not explained, at the time of these events Mr Margetts was staying at the Cooch family home, and kept his own linen there. Whilst working at the house, Susannah received news that her younger sister, Mary, had died on 22 October, and she needed to go back home at once.

She packed her boxes to go. We are not told why Mr Cooch became suspicious as to the contents of her luggage, but he was suspicious, and he asked her to open her boxes up so that he could inspect the contents.

Inside, he found a shirt, two tablecloths, two dinner napkins, five sheets, two towels, two diapers, a bolster case and two handkerchiefs, all of which belonged to him. He also found a skirt, two pairs of gold wristband links, a gold chain and key, six pairs of socks, three nightshirts, fifteen collars and two shirts, all the property of his neighbour, Robert Margetts (although no one explained why Mr Margetts had a skirt). This was a bold haul: there can hardly have been much room left for her own things.

The trial was not given much attention in the local press (despite the skirt), and it is necessary to look further afield to the newspaper that served the area of Susannah's birth to find a fuller account. Her family resided at Weston Longville, and they must have felt the blast of the publicity in their local press. On the day of the trial, it seems that her very large family had mustered a crowd to attend at Huntingdon in her support, and the case had excited a lot of local interest, too.

The press report described her as being a good-looking woman, then aged twenty-nine, and as being very well-dressed.[lviii] She had managed to instruct a solicitor and a barrister to represent her on the day. Her counsel is said to have made a most impressive speech on her behalf, and it is a shame that fuller details of it do not survive, because no doubt the reader would be fascinated to know what could be said to improve the impression that arises from the facts themselves.

It is said to have been based on her rush to pack following the distressing news of her sister's death: she had merely placed the things into her box intending to put them away properly on her return after the funeral, and had no intention of stealing them. The jury took almost no time at all to acquit her on the first count, of theft from Mr Cooch. There was a great deal of cheering from her family in the court room, which was suppressed immediately by the judge.

The second case was conducted entirely separately, but consisted of similar evidence, this time in relation to the articles belonging to Mr Margetts. The jury acquitted her a second time.

The chairman of the bench gave her some very useful advice for the future: she should avoid putting other people's property into her boxes. This suggests that he was not entirely comfortable with the verdict.[lix]

After this, Susannah was not prevented from obtaining another position in service. Indeed, she seems to have taken a decided step up in the hierarchy by the 1871 census, because she appears in the household of a retired colonel of the Indian Army, at a smart address in Chelsea, as lady's maid. At some point whilst she was living in London, she met a carpenter from Yorkshire named William Dobinson, and when they were both about thirty-seven, they married. They had a small family – just three children, which was perhaps a deliberate choice on Susannah's part.

*38 Waggon & Horses, Catworth.*

# George Hailes carries it off: Catworth, December 1868

George was born in about 1850. At the date of his offences, he was aged eighteen, and was working as a carrier (or deliveryman), in Catworth. This was a very responsible job: it involved people trusting you with their goods – business and personal – for carriage to and from local towns and villages. A carrier had to be completely trustworthy and above suspicion, or his business was worthless.

George was charged with having stolen a long list of items. Although he might have had the opportunity to steal or tamper with parcels that he carried as part of his trade, the offences for which he was arrested were all straightforward opportunistic thefts, and shop-lifting. The items he took were as follows:

28 November, from the Rev. John Bell at the rectory in Brington: three shoe brushes; two silver tablespoons; two silver teaspoons; two silver dinner forks.

28 November, from the Catworth shop of Mr Henry Smith: collars, braces, buttons, a door spring, a sponge, some leggings and 2 1/2 yards of merino wool cloth.

2$^{nd}$ December from John Ingrams' shop in Huntingdon: ink, bulbs and seeds.

39 *Bringtom Rectory, about 1900.*

George took some of the items to Huntingdon and tried to persuade another trader to give him money for them, but the man was suspicious and didn't fall for it.

George wrote to his friend, Hannah Brown, who was in service at a house in Great Haddington, sending her the merino cloth and the spoons, telling her that they were a gift following the death of his grandmother. She does not appear to have believed him.

It was the door spring that started the investigation that led to his downfall: PC Bland at Catworth had obtained a warrant to arrest him on suspicion of its theft and, when he got to George's lodgings, he searched his box and found many of the other stolen articles in it.

George gave the constable the usual story: he had bought the things from a 'cheap Jack' at Thrapston, but had no idea who the man was. Hannah handed in the items she had received, including Rev. Bell's silver cutlery. George was a frequent visitor to the rectory in Brington, bringing deliveries or collecting parcels, and had obviously seized an opportunity to pick up more than he was entitled to.

John Ingram was a nurseryman in Huntingdon. George had called at his shop on 2 December to pay a bill and to place an order. The assistant had had to leave him alone in the shop for a short time, and whilst he was away, George had helped himself to the ink and seeds and to some hyacinth and tulip bulbs.

At his trial, George pleaded guilty, and had nothing whatsoever to say to the jury.

He was sentenced to eighteen months' imprisonment, with hard labour.

Unfortunately, it did not take very long before he felt an overwhelming need to get out of the gaol. On the night of 19 January 1869, he tried to escape by getting out of a window. When his attempt failed, he tried instead to cut his own throat with a piece of the broken glass. He certainly did succeed in making a very nasty cut to his throat, but realising the danger he was in, he called out for help, and the prison staff managed to get a surgeon to attend to him in time to save his life.[lx]

Hannah Brown, a young lady of similar age to George, had been born and raised in Catworth. George regarded her as his sweetheart, but whether she returned his affections is unknown. She had a position of responsibility as a servant in a respectable household: a person's name and character were everything. She really had had no choice but to hand George's 'gifts' over to the police to avoid being implicated in receiving stolen goods.

40 *Catworth post office.*

41 *St Neots Market Square.*

On 15 November that year Hannah married Mr Samuel Smith, a farmworker from Northamptonshire. Perhaps this was already in the air when George had plied her with the silver spoons, and it had been a desperate attempt to win her back.

George seems to have managed to get through the rest of his sentence without further adventures, but encountered a hiccup just as he was being discharged from the gaol: evidence had come to light in the meantime of another theft, this time of glassware and china from a delivery that had arrived at Tilbrook station around the time of the earlier thefts.[lxi] The timing was very unfortunate. No sooner had he stepped out of the gaol than he was rearrested, and brought before the magistrates in Huntingdon. They were short of a witness or two, and were unable to proceed, and they therefore postponed the matter to a later date to allow the witnesses to attend. It seems, however, that the matter was then just dropped. How George earned his living after this is not known.

## Regular reports on Huntingdon Gaol

Huntingdon Gaol performed an essential community service, and the public was interested in how it was run. Its management was open to public scrutiny in a way that might find surprising today.

At each sitting of the quarter sessions, the court would receive a report from a committee of justices of the peace known as 'the visiting justices', whose duty it was to inspect the gaol and assess the state of discipline, the financial accounts and the morals and morale of both prisoners and the staff.

At the same time, the quarter sessions would receive a surgeon's report on the health of the inmates over the past quarter, with details of any infectious diseases, a chaplain's report, the gaol-keeper's report containing statistics on the gaol population and expenditure, and a report from the chief constable on the state of crime generally in the area. These were published in the press, and ensured accountability of those responsible for the welfare of prison inmates. The rate-payers of Huntingdonshire could see how much was being spent on keeping prisoners in gaol, and could see whether the sum per head was going up or down.

Male inmates were always significantly in the majority. There was no separate accommodation for female prisoners until after 1864. The prison held those who had been sentenced for both serious and minor offences, some civil debtors who, of course, were guilty of no crime as such; those who were merely remanded pending a trial at which they might be acquitted and leave the penal system altogether, and 'vagrants' – those who, when challenged to do so, could not provide satisfactory evidence of a permanent address.

In 1872 the report given was short and to the point:

> *The Report of the Visiting Justices and of the Governor of the Gaol showed that there was a much smaller number of prisoners in the gaol than usual, and the sentences of all would expire by the 12th instant, so that unless some more were sent before that day the gaol would be empty. A large decrease of trivial and indictable offences was also reported, as well as a further extraordinary decrease of vagrancy.*

By the following year, there was concern for the rising cost of feeding the inmates:

> *The Visiting Justices reported a considerable increase in the gaol expenses owing to a rise in the price of most articles required, particularly of oatmeal, potatoes, coals, and gas. The cost of dietary per head was 5 ¼d. The use of Australian meat had been under consideration for some time, and the Secretary of State had now sanctioned its use provided that an addition of one sixth be made to each ration to make up for the overcooking which it undergoes in the present mode of preserving it.*[lxii]

# The Parson' Horse and the Windmill: Inventive justice, Huntingdon 1807

In 1807, a civil matter erupted in Huntingdon that caused a great deal of local excitement and upset, and at the same time made legal history.

Enclosure of common land occurred throughout the country by successive Acts of Parliament, entitling local commissioners to make 'awards' of what had formerly been common grazing and agricultural land, so that it came under the control of private individuals. It was sometimes necessary to create new roads (called 'enclosure roads') at the same time, in order to maintain sufficient access to the new parcels of land created by this process.

In in this particular case, a miller had long had his windmill in the middle of some common land, but following the enclosure of the common, the commissioners had found it necessary to create an enclosure road which, unfortunately, passed right under the 'fly' (i.e. the sails) of his mill. He had absolutely no choice in the matter.

The result of this state of affairs was that people were now required to pass beneath the sails of the mill if they wished to cross the land to get from A to B. Sadly, the several reports of this case that appeared across the country do not tell us the identity either of these geographical points nor of the parties, as the point of law itself was the main focus of the national interest.

What happens when you ride your horse underneath a windmill, and the sails start up? Well, unless your horse is particularly well-trained (or blind) it is likely to result in the rider being unseated, or possibly carried off at a gallop. This happened to a local parson (said to be a man of considerable property in the neighbourhood) so many times that he had had quite enough of it, and had the miller indicted for public nuisance endangering the lives of His Majesty's citizens.

The judge was in a quandary. It was his task to address the jury and to sum up for them the legal arguments for both sides, and assist them to apply the law to the facts before them. He told them that on the facts, it was impossible to conclude otherwise than that the mill constituted a public nuisance. But, on the other hand, the miller was not to blame for the predicament in which he found himself. The judge therefore directed the jury that the facts required that they should find the miller guilty, and so they did.

When considering the penalty, the judge said that the requirement for fairness dictated that the poor miller should not be punished for something over which he had no control. The clergyman who had brought the case, on the other hand, was a very rich man, but deserved justice. He therefore broke new legal ground: he ordered that the prosecuting clergyman should pay the defendant miller the (in those days) eyewatering sum of £40, and that the miller should be ordered to use it to abate the nuisance, and should also be awarded the right to move his mill onto a convenient adjoining site.[lxiii]

This little piece of creativity was the first time that a court had been known to order the winning plaintiff to pay the defendant, but the judge was lauded for his originality and the appropriateness of the outcome (although probably not by the clergyman).

# Why young boys should not be left in charge of guns: Luke Parker, Folksworth, August 1811

This was a really dreadful tragedy, caused by the recklessness of a group of very naughty boys at Stilton. Today, it would be unthinkable (in this country) to allow young children to be in charge of a loaded gun, but there was nothing in the law to prohibit anyone, of any age, from owning or handling a gun kind when these events happened.

In July 1811, a ten-year-old boy named Thomas Cave had been put in charge of a gun by his father, who wished him to stand in his pea field in Folksworth and use it to ward off the birds. This was high summer: the pea crop was nearing readiness for harvest, and was at its most vulnerable. Thomas's duties attracted a number of other lads from the village, who were only too happy to keep him company, and they all took turns shooting at a mark to while away the time.

On the morning of 25 July, two young girls from the village, Rebecca Sykes (aged six) and Georgiana Rowell (aged ten), needed to use a footpath across the field in order to get to school. Thomas and some of his friends were in the field, cutting up a piece of lead (we will not enquire where they got it from), and as the girls went by, they said that if they tried to cross the field again on their way back from school, they would shoot them.

The two girls were sufficiently scared of the boys that when it was time to come back home, they called on their thirteen-year-old friend, Elizabeth Kirkby, who was in service at a house near to the school. They asked her mistress if she would allow Elizabeth to walk home with them, and Elizabeth was given leave to go with them.

As they approached the field, they saw Thomas with another boy, Luke Parker. Luke, who was nine, lived at the Bell Inn at Stilton with his father, who was employed there. The two boys were standing near to the stile at the entrance of the field. Luke called out that if the girls tried to get over the stile, he would shoot them. Rebecca told him that her father would horse whip him if he made them climb over the gate, and she wasn't going to do it just to please him. She and Georgiana were in favour of going the long way round, but Elizabeth refused to give way. Luke said that he would shoot her, but Thomas told him not to, or they would both be hanged. Luke replied to

Thomas that he only meant to frighten them, and he aimed the gun and pulled the trigger. Elizabeth took the full force of the bullet through her right cheek and straight through her head.

The boys were absolutely terrified. They ran away, leaving Rebecca and Georgiana helplessly trying to attend to their friend. Thomas then came running back, crying, and asked whether it was his fault that it had happened. The local baker, who happened to be coming up the lane, was first on the scene, but could do nothing to save Elizabeth's life.

Luke was overcome with distress. He and Thomas were both arrested, and kept in custody in Huntingdon gaol until the outcome of the inquest, which was held the following day. The inquest found that Elizabeth's death had been caused by manslaughter on the part of Luke, and that Thomas had aided and abetted it.

The boys came before the Huntingdon assizes a few days later, and it was lucky for them that the events had taken place so close to the date when the assizes were sitting, or they could have spent several months longer locked up. The court was full to overflowing with local people who were of course very interested in the case.

The grand jury decided very quickly that there was no case to answer on the part of Thomas, and he was discharged. In relation to Luke, however, they found a 'true bill', not for manslaughter, but for murder, and so he was sent for trial at once.

The prosecutor made the point that the jury would find the extreme youth of this small defendant very affecting. Luke's position was lamentable, but the only matter for decision was whether they believed that at the moment when he pulled the trigger, he really intended to cause death or serious injury. If they believed that it was merely 'wanton, thoughtless and indiscreet', then it would not be murder.

In Luke's defence, two character witnesses were called. The first was Mr Gibbs, the owner of the Bell Inn where his father was employed. The second was Mr Bodge, their landlord. They both reported that Luke was a 'quiet, inoffensive and tractable' boy, and by no means given to mischief.

The jury took only a very few minutes to decide that he was not guilty of murder.

Nothing certain can be found about poor Elizabeth or her family. Luke seems to have come to terms with what happened sufficiently to remain in Stilton, where he eventually became a plumber and glazier, and married a local girl. He remained in Stilton until his death there in 1877.

# Mrs Scarborough would like you to know that she is innocent: Buckden, 1818

Here is a moving story of an undoubted miscarriage of justice.

Jane Scarborough and her husband, John, owned the George Inn at Buckden. Mr Scarborough also owned a substantial farm in the village, so that the day-to-day management of the inn fell to Jane.

The couple had lived in the village for over twenty years at the date of these events, and had brought up two sons and four daughters there 'in the path of virtue and of industry'.[lxiv] They were held in great esteem by their neighbours and associates: they settled their accounts as they fell due; they ran a good business, and enjoyed the patronage of many eminent persons at their inn, including his Royal Highness the Prince Regent.

In 1814, the opportunity to purchase the Bell Inn at Stilton had come up, and they had decided to take it. It had been left vacant for some time, and this had seriously threatened their own business in Buckden: the Bell was the next 'post house' in the line along the Great North Road en route to London, and without it being kept afoot there was a danger that the stage route would be diverted via other inns, and they would lose 'the line'. Mrs Scarborough invested £1000 of her own private fortune into the business on behalf of her son, John, whom they set up as innkeeper.

After some ups and downs (and some dirty tricks by the keeper of the Angel Inn, opposite, who tried to divert custom from the Bell in a most underhand way), the business in Stilton seemed to be going satisfactorily. Jane Scarborough frequently attended at the Bell to assist her son in the business there.

The vicar of Buckden, the Rev. Dr Maltby, used to run a tutoring business for the sons of the gentry, and to this end up to half a dozen or so young gentlemen would be residing at the rectory with the Maltbys from time to time. Dr Maltby included amongst his pupils the subsequently famous Edward Bouverie Pusey.

In 1815, the son of Richard Preston, MP for Ashburton in Devon, studied at the rectory with Dr Maltby for about six months before going up to Cambridge. This young man was the indirect cause of the miserable events in this story.

42 *Buckden, about 1908, with the George Inn on the left, and the Lion & Lamb on the right.*

The boy's father wished to send him some money through the post, to which end he had directed his secretary to place a £20 note into an envelope with a letter addressed to his son at Dr Maltby's house, in Buckden. The secretary was sufficiently cautious to have made a note of the serial number of the £20 note before he committed it to the post, and this was the means, later, of identifying the particular note in question.

The money did not arrive. There is a little doubt whether the letter arrived but without the note, or whether the entire envelope was missing. The impression given at the trial was that the letter simply was not delivered.

Mr Preston caused enquiries to be carried out by the post office, and many individuals were interviewed as to the fate of the letter. During these enquiries, Mr Cox, the postmaster at Buckden, said that he was absolutely sure that every letter sent up to Buckden from Huntingdon on the day in question had been duly delivered.

Much later – in fact more than a year later, and, it seems, after some heavy prompting from Dr Maltby – Mr Cox 'remembered' that around that time he had had one letter that was very blotted and blotched, so that he had been unable to read the address on it. He had taken it to Jane Scarborough at the George Inn, to ask her if she could make out the address. He said that she had told him she knew the addressee, and if he left it with her, she would ensure it

43 *The George, Buckden.*

was delivered. The following day, he said, he had checked with her, and she had confirmed to him that she had ensured it had been taken to the proper recipient. Despite being postmaster, he does not seem to have bothered to ask her to whom she had delivered it.

Shortly after the date when the letter should have arrived, Jane Scarborough had gone to stay for several days at the Bell Inn, to help out whilst her son was away on business. Whilst she was there, a carriage had arrived at the inn, in which a man and two women were travelling together. They wanted to change their horses and to be straight on their way, so did not step inside the inn. When the man was ready to pay for the horses, he enquired whether Jane would be able to give him change for a £20 note. She had no difficulty in doing so, as she had a large roll of notes (including several £20 notes) in her purse as a result of takings from the inn, and so she accepted the note from him and gave him change.

One of the reasons for her attendance at the Bell at that time was that she had agreed to supervise the settlement of a debt owed by her son, to which end both her son's attorney and the attorney of the creditor were due to come to the inn in order that the repayment could be properly documented. When the relevant parties were all assembled (shortly after the business with the man who had just changed his horses), Jane paid the sum of £48 and some shillings

44 *Stilton, showing both the Bell Inn and the Angel Inn.*

to her attorney, taking the notes at random from the bundle of cash that she was holding in her hand. She gave him a £20 note, a £10 note, three £5 notes and three £1 notes. Her attorney passed the same money to Mr Bond, the attorney of the creditor, who placed the notes in his pocket-book.

From this moment onward, the journey of the £20 note thus given to Mr Bond was given in court as follows:

After receiving the £20 note, Mr Bond was sure that he did not remove it from his pocket-book until he handed it to Mr Price, a printer from Leicester.

Mr Price, immediately on receipt of the money, mailed it to a wholesale stationer, in London.

On receipt of it, the stationer passed it to his clerk, who wrote Mr Price's name on the note, in order to record that the payment was his. Thus, at the end of this laborious passage, there should have existed a £20 bearing the name of Mr Price, representing the very note handed by Jane Scarborough to her attorney.

The problem was that when the £20 was paid into the bank by the stationer's clerk, the bank raised the alarm, because it was by now on their 'stolen' list as representing Mr Preston's missing money.

Enquiries persisted, and as the note was traced back to Jane at Stilton, she was merely asked to account for how she had come by it. She gave the account of the gentleman who had asked her to change a £20 note at the Bell. Nobody informed her that the note was stolen property; she assumed that the authorities were interested in it because it had turned out to be a forgery. She believed that if that was the case, she would be liable to make up the value of it to Mr Bond, to whom it had been paid on her son's behalf, and although she was not very happy about that, she would have been able to stand the loss.

Dr Maltby seems to have worn several hats in this tale. As Mrs Scarborough's friend, he had been in the habit of consulting her on many day-to-day topics, and gave every appearance of valuing her judgement. As a patron of her establishment, he kept a yearly 'tab' for his horses. It was not as either a friend or a patron, however, that he dropped her a note inviting her to call in at his house at an appointed date and time, without informing her of true purport of the meeting. The hat he was wearing on this occasion was that of a magistrate.

He had, in fact, gathered together various parties at his house to conduct an examination of the evidence, and to her utter shock, the outcome was that she was charged with the theft of the note, and was immediately committed to trial at Huntingdon Assizes. She was required on the spot to furnish the magistrate with two sureties in the sum of £200 apiece to secure her attendance at court, failing which she would have been taken away to prison. She was utterly distraught.

Her own family lawyer tried to assist in the early stages of the matter, but was located just too far away to be of real assistance to her. He advised her to instruct a local lawyer, and she therefore arranged to be represented by Mr Wells, of Huntingdon. She later seriously regretted this decision.

Her case was due to be heard at the Lent assizes in 1817, but on the day of the hearing the prosecution reported that, due to a mistake on their part, they had been unable to obtain the presence of one of the stationers, who was regarded as a key witness. As a result, the case was postponed to the summer assizes, and Jane's distress was thus extended for several more months. She found the intervening months very difficult to bear.

Finally, she came before the court in the August of 1817. Mr Wells had assured her that the grand jury would be highly unlikely to find a 'true bill' and that the most likely outcome was that the case would be thrown out without a trial. This did not happen: the jury did find a true bill, and the case went forward for an immediate hearing. There were many witnesses called for both sides, and the hearing lasted over six hours.

45 *Buckden, the Bishop's Palace and St Mary's Church.*

The trial evidence was rather complicated. In order to pin the crime onto Mrs Scarborough, it was necessary for the prosecution to prove that the letter containing the money for Mr Preston's son had arrived in the proper course of the post, but had been handled by her at some point after its arrival in Buckden, when she had had the opportunity to pocket it.

This entailed calling a string of witnesses in the employ of the postal service, to prove that the item would have been collected by a letter-handler, taken to the post office in London, placed onto the train to the nearest sorting office in Huntingdon, bagged up for delivery to Buckden and then taken to the Buckden postmaster, William Cox.

Given this chain of evidence today, it would be a poor advocate indeed who did not make a sterling defence out of the many junctures at which it was impossible to say that the letter in question was in this bag, that mail coach or that sack. It was all highly circumstantial, as none of these witnesses pretended to be able to recall this specific letter.

In accordance with the rules of the time, Jane Scarborough's counsel was not permitted to address the jury on her behalf. In her own defence, however, Mrs Scarborough entered a written statement, read out to the jury, in which she referred to her good character and reputation, and denied ever having handled the missing letter.

There then followed no fewer than eleven character witnesses for Mrs Scarborough, some of whom, it was said, were 'of the first condition in the country'. They included names we will recognise today as prominent in the locality: Sir James Duberly of Gaines Hall, George Thornhill of Diddington, Lawrence Reynolds, William Day and several others. The Lord Bishop of Lincoln (her neighbour at Buckden Palace) could not attend in person but sent a written testimonial of her excellent character. All of them confirmed Mrs Scarborough's thorough and absolute honesty. Dr Maltby himself stood as a character witness for her, despite having been one of the magistrates who had charged her and committed her for trial.

The judge, in his summing-up to the jury, advised them that evidence of good character carried no weight if the evidence against the defendant was felt to be clear. If they felt the evidence was unclear, the evidence of her previous good character could be allowed to influence their decision.

Unfortunately for Jane, after considering the matter for about an hour, the jury found the evidence against her clear enough, and they found her guilty. She was sentenced to a year in prison, which the judge said was a lighter sentence than he might otherwise pass, in consideration of her previous good character. Jane was taken away to prison, protesting her innocence as she went.

Her attorney had not prepared her for this outcome. Her distress was overwhelming. She was taken by carriage to Huntingdon gaol, and was allowed to have her daughter stay with her on her first night. Afterwards, she found some comfort from the fact that there were two women in the gaol who were known to her – a Mrs Smith, who was incarcerated for debt, and another woman also from Buckden. These two ladies supported Jane in her grief and did their best to console her. She was permitted to share what she later called 'an apartment' with them, but they were in due course released when their terms of imprisonment came to an end, after which she was on her own.

She appears to have received considerate treatment from the governor of the gaol. She was permitted visits three times a week from her family, and they made these visits no matter what the weather, bringing with them food and other necessities to maintain her. It appears to have been a matter of pride on Jane's part that she accepted no sustenance from 'the county' whilst serving her sentence, but was entirely supported by her family. Somehow, she got through this ordeal, and at the end of twelve months she was restored to her family.

Her reputation, however, needed a little work.

She was still burning with anger at the injustice she had suffered, and had had plenty of time to think it all over whilst she was in prison.

Mr Wells, her attorney, had failed to call what she considered to be two key witnesses, who could have cast doubt on the evidence of Mr Cox, the postmaster who had managed to convince the jury that he had put the fateful letter into her hands.

One was a friend of the family, to whom Mr Cox had made a statement contradicting the evidence he had given in court; the other was a young man who was then at Cambridge University with Mr Preston's son, and to whom Preston Jnr had said that he had, in fact, received a letter from his father on the day in question, but there had been no money inside. This latter evidence would have suggested an entirely different sequence of events, perhaps being that Mr Preston's secretary had failed to enclose £20 note in the first place. Both of these pieces of testimony had been referred to Mr Wells beforehand, but he had failed to follow it up or to call the men to give evidence.

She considered that he had been seriously negligent in the way he had prepared and presented her case, and whilst she also believed the jury to have been either malign or ignorant, she considered Mr Wells to be principally responsible for the appalling experience of the loss of her reputation and her sentence of imprisonment.

She was also especially bitter about the treatment she had received from Dr Maltby. They had been neighbours, and she had regarded him as a friend. He had known her as an honest and respectable woman of means for over twenty years. He had concealed from her the fact that she was under suspicion until it was too late for her to bring forward witnesses who could have countered the allegations at the meeting held at his house. The matter could have been stopped before it had started. He seems to have run with the hare and hunted with the hounds, in that he connived to have her charged, but later testified to her excellent character, in court. If this suggests a man who knew how to hedge his bets, it may not come as a surprise to learn that he was an ardent politician in his spare time.

For Jane, the consequences of her conviction were sadly far-reaching. Business at the George Inn suffered badly. In due course, the family lost the George, the Bell and the farm, and all their possessions. Both her husband and her son were made bankrupt.[lxv] Jane herself had invested all her personal fortune into the Bell, and was left penniless.

They left the area shortly after she was released from prison, and one of Jane's first actions was to publish notices in the press, maintaining her

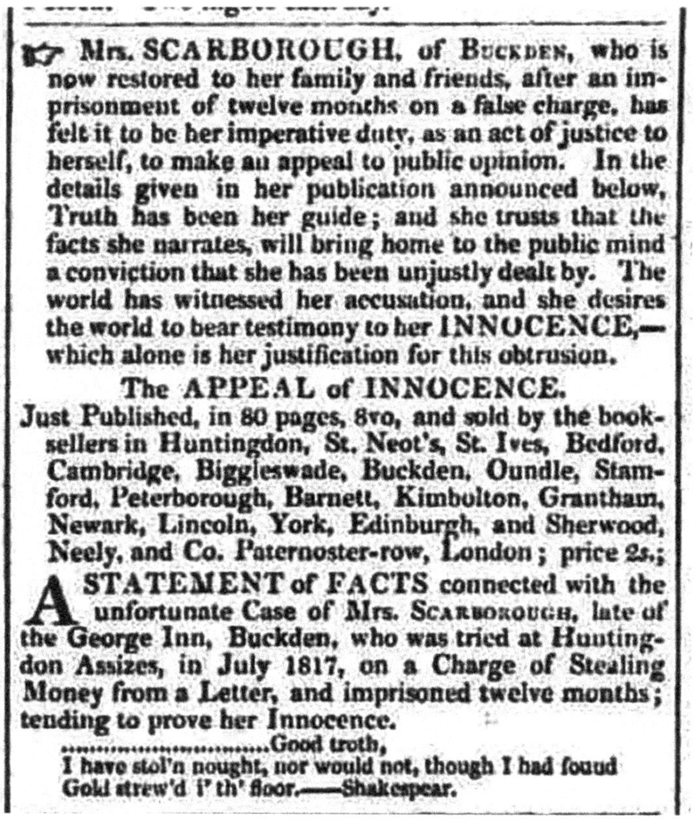

☞ Mrs. SCARBOROUGH, of BUCKDEN, who is now restored to her family and friends, after an imprisonment of twelve months on a false charge, has felt it to be her imperative duty, as an act of justice to herself, to make an appeal to public opinion. In the details given in her publication announced below, Truth has been her guide; and she trusts that the facts she narrates, will bring home to the public mind a conviction that she has been unjustly dealt by. The world has witnessed her accusation, and she desires the world to bear testimony to her INNOCENCE,—which alone is her justification for this obtrusion.

The APPEAL of INNOCENCE.

Just Published, in 80 pages, 8vo, and sold by the booksellers in Huntingdon, St. Neot's, St. Ives, Bedford, Cambridge, Biggleswade, Buckden, Oundle, Stamford, Peterborough, Barnett, Kimbolton, Grantham, Newark, Lincoln, York, Edinburgh, and Sherwood, Neely, and Co. Paternoster-row, London; price 2s.;

A STATEMENT of FACTS connected with the unfortunate Case of Mrs. SCARBOROUGH, late of the George Inn, Buckden, who was tried at Huntingdon Assizes, in July 1817, on a Charge of Stealing Money from a Letter, and imprisoned twelve months; tending to prove her Innocence.

.............................Good troth,
I have stol'n nought, nor would not, though I had found
Gold strew'd i' th' floor.——Shakespear.

46 *Mrs Scarborough's appeal to the public.*

innocence. She wrote and published a full account of the trial and of her sufferings.

Destitute, they moved to Windlesham in Surrey, where John took the licence of the Kings Arms Inn. He kept the inn until his death in 1825, and from that year forward until her own death in 1834, Jane took over the running of the business.

During this period of time, did Dr Maltby think of the Scarborough family and consider their plight?

He began to expect clerical preferment in the years following these events, but despite various vacancies occurring, he was repeatedly disappointed for a number of years in his hope of being elevated to the position of bishop, despite his political profile.

47 *Rev. Dr Edward Maltby. An impressive monument to his first wife can be seen in St Mary's Church, Buckden.*

In 1827, the Manchester Courier published a scathing comment on his apparent status as a renowned scholar of Greek:

> *The Doctor [. . .] is one of those heavy grinders who obtain the reputation of being scholars, by perpetually dabbling in Greek, without understanding one Greek author, and continually giving out that they are very learned. What Parr was to Porson, Maltby is to Parr – a lower flight of heavy literary day-labourer, without a particle of taste, genius, or real learning. His claim on promotion is, we suppose, his whiggery.* [lxvi]

It was at least in part his 'whiggery' that finally won him his promotion. As a result of his outspoken Whig politics, his party (who were in power at the time) were anxious to accelerate his promotion to the House of Lords, in order to try to establish the majority they desperately needed in that house, and which kept them from being able to pass their parliamentary bills.

48 *Auckland Castle, the home of Dr Maltby from 1837.*

When the Bishop of Worcester died in 1831, a multi-partite clerical reshuffle was executed at the speed of light, resulting in Dr Maltby taking possession of the Bishop's Palace in Winchester before his brother bishop had even been buried. This caused a public scandal, but it appears that so long as the keys to the palace gates had been handed over, everything else was water off a duck's back.

The reason for the haste was entirely strategic. The Whig Reform Bill was due to be debated in the Lords in the first week of October, and the party needed all the votes it could muster.

In 1837, Maltby was made Bishop of Durham. In that position, he took up residence at Auckland Castle, which he no doubt found exceedingly comfortable.

In due course, the honour fell to the mitred Maltby to hand the royal orb to Queen Victoria at her coronation ceremony. Jane Scarborough (if she had not already relinquished all earthly cares) could have taken a little sadistic pleasure in learning that, by mistake, he threw the ball to the Queen at the wrong moment, and that his new sovereign pronounced him to be '*remarkably maladroit*'.

49 *Dr Maltby's dropped ball.*[lxvii]

# A snapshot of the Huntingdon Summer Assizes, 1826

Thomas Marshall, for stealing two sheep from John Nix of Little Raveley – death.

James Johnson, for taking a cotton handkerchief from the pocket of William Dunmore in Huntingdon: transportation for life.

James Rogers and Henry Robinson, for stealing John Piggott's breeches from a fence in Hartford Lane, Huntingdon: three months imprisonment with hard labour.[lxviii]

# Symptoms of innocence: Lent Assizes, Huntingdon, 1827

Immediately after a man was found not guilty of horse-stealing at the Huntingdon assizes, he left the court and, speaking of the principal witness in the case, observed with indignation: 'What a d****d lie that fellow told! We never took the horse through the town at all!'[lxix]

# The prisoners' conditions

The yearly returns of the Huntingdon visiting magistrates were collated with all the returns from the other prisons across the country, and published annually in a parliamentary report, enabling comparisons to be made. Huntingdon gaol, on the whole, achieved a lower cost per capita for feeding and clothing its inmates than most other English gaols. The number of hours for which the inmates were set to the treadmill was about average. Each gaol had to give a detailed breakdown of the 'hard labour' to which it put its convicts. The following figures for Huntingdon given in 1848 were roughly average when compared with other gaols:

Average hours spent on the treadwheel: 8 ¾.

Height of treadwheel steps: 8 inches.

Average number of steps achieved per minute: 48.

Average height climbed per day: 16,500 feet.

Purpose of treadwheel: to grind corn.

The diet and clothing of the prisoners at Huntingdon was not described, but at nearby Bedford in 1842, full details of the diet were given:[lxx]

**New Dietary ordered by Visiting Justices on the 28th February, 1842.**

*Prisoners before Trial.*

A meat dumpling, consisting of three ounces of meat and eight ounces of flour on Monday, Wednesday, and Friday, in lieu of the suet pudding, in addition to two pounds of bread, and on alternate days, two pounds of bread, two ounces of cheese, and an onion.

*Prisoners confined under three Months.*

Two pounds of bread, two ounces of cheese, and an onion five days in the week, and on Tuesday and Saturday one pint of soup, and two pounds of bread.

*Prisoners above Three Months and under Six Months.*

A meat pudding, consisting of three ounces of meat and eight ounces of flour on Monday, Wednesday, and Friday, in addition to two pounds of bread, and on alternate days, two pounds of bread, two ounces of cheese, an onion, and one pint of beer on Tuesday and Saturday.

*Prisoners above Six Months and under Twelve Months.*

A meat pudding, consisting of four ounces of meat and eight ounces of flour, on Monday Wednesday, and Friday, in addition to two pounds of bread, and on alternate days, two pounds of bread, two ounces of cheese, an onion, and one pint of beer.

*Prisoners above Twelve Months.*

A meat pudding, consisting of four ounces of meat and eight ounces of flour, on Sunday, Monday, Wednesday, and Friday, with two pounds of bread; and on Tuesday, Thursday, and Saturday, two pounds of bread, two ounces of cheese, and an onion; and a pint of beer on Sunday, Tuesday, Thursday, and Saturday.

## The well-destroyer of Hilton: George Goodman Hewett, 1829

Mr Hewett was a notorious complainer. Originally a Norfolk man, and a surgeon of some considerable financial means, he had made his home in the village of Hilton after a rather interesting career.

He had participated in the longest recorded Pacific voyage – some four years in length – in the company of Captain George Vancouver, who had been with Captain Cook on his last and fatal voyage. Indeed, Hewett was later on board the *Discovery* herself, in the capacity of surgeon's mate.

Vancouver (and George) sailed in 1791 in search of the North West Passage. Vancouver was regarded by his crew and officers as something of a tyrant, but his insistence on good diet had resulted in his medical team having relatively little to do. Perhaps for this reason, Hewett had had time to amass what was later acknowledged to be one of the most extensive collections of ethnic artefacts of any explorer of the eighteenth century, and the collection was destined (after some adventures of its own) for the British Museum. He was, therefore, a man with some kudos, stature and esteem, and not at all the kind of man to overlook irresponsible spending on the part of his parish.

As a rate-payer, he made it his business to quibble continually over the parish accounts, and to argue with the councillors over how the parish spent its money. The members of the council received plenty of advice from him, but did not often follow it. It was said that the parish council liked the doctor's advice even less than they liked his medicine.

He frequently took his allegations of financial misbehaviour to the magistrates, whose role it was in those days to oversee the exercise of the parish council's administrative functions. It is fair to say that he was not a popular man.

In a deeply deplorable outbreak of puerility, it seems that some parish council members encouraged the composing of a number of very silly and insulting ballads about Mr Hewett, and had them performed up and down the street outside his house.

A certain Mr Hodge was observed by Mr Hewett to have had a particularly high profile during these musical performances, and to have sung to very large crowds, to the extent that the angry surgeon decided he must be the ring-leader. He surprised no one by commencing a libel action against Mr Hodge.

One of the creations was a musical setting of the village's opinion of a particularly unpopular piece of work on the part of the surgeon. As a result of pressure from a Mr Theed, the parish council had permitted the sinking of a water well on a public highway in order to provide fresh drinking water to some poor cottagers, who had previously been without that privilege. Mr Hewett and, it must in fairness be said, others, had objected that it was on public land. In due course, the official surveyor of the highways had had no choice but to agree that it should be filled in. The filling-in of the well, which was of course a great pity for the poor cottagers, was regarded as symbolic of Mr Hewett's oppression of the residents of Hilton, and the hostility of a portion of the villagers was naturally thereby increased.

The reader might here like to inspect the content of two of the ballads – which are saucy rather than accomplished – and to consider whether it would be likely to trigger a libel action today:

Lines written by a lady of Hilton who loves good water:

*God gave us water, Theed made it good*
*Hewett took it from us, God d**n his blood!*
*The devil is dead, and Hell will rue it:*
*His friend succeeds him – George Goodman Hewett!*
*Alas poor Hilton, how you'll rue it*
*If you are governed by G. G. Hewett!*

And:

*There is a man in Hilton whose name I do not mention*
*Who would destroy poor people's water, it is his full intention;*
*He is called the old informer, it a scandalous name,*
*He would do any mischief for the lucre of gain.*
*If this rogue into limbo*[9] *should get,*
*For straying people's water, it would shew him a trick*
*The rich would rejoice, and the poor would sing,*
*For straying a well of water, it is a great sin.*[lxxi]

When Mr Hodge came before the assizes to answer the charge, he took with him a printed copy of these two ballads, and cheekily told the court that he understood that Mr Hewett had been asking for a copy, and that he could have them for five shillings. He pointed out that he had not written the material himself, he had merely entertained the crowds at the Red Cow Inn and handed them out to the crowd at the blacksmith's barn.

In Hodge's defence, his counsel argued that the matter was far from serious, and that if any offence had been caused by the doggerel verses, Mr Hewett had brought it on himself by his officious meddling in village affairs.

Unfortunately, the jury disagreed, and found him guilty. He was sentenced to pay a fine of £5 and to provide two sureties of £50 each to keep the peace for a year.

Mr Hewett died in 1834, having made good use of the intervening five years by instituting many more actions against his fellow villagers, in which he

[9] Limbo here means purgatory.

represented himself, without legal assistance, he having by that time probably more experience than most lawyers.

Despite his celebrity (or perhaps because of it), the local press was unusually silent on the matter of his passing. Obituaries of prominent or well-known persons in the locality would invariably be considered worthy to be printed, but not, it seems for George Hewett. Someone must have pointed this out to the Huntingdon, Bedford & Peterborough Gazette, because the week afterwards, the paper (whose motto was 'Nothing extenuate, nor set down aught in malice')[10] included the following in their weekly round-up of events:

'We omitted to state in our last the death of Mr Hewett, of Hilton.'[lxxii]

Here, 'less' was decidedly 'more'.

## Taking a test drive too far: John Smith (aka John Wilks), October 1828

John Stracey kept the White Hart Inn in Godmanchester, and he had a mare for sale. A Mr Smith said that he was interested in buying it, and after some discussion had taken place between them about the price, Mr Smith said that he would like to give the horse a little try-out before he made up his mind.

Up hopped Mr Smith into the saddle, and he gently walked the mare along the road for some 150 yards, and then he suddenly broke into a frenzied gallop and disappeared over the horizon. It occurred to Mr Stracey that this did not look quite right.

Mr Stracey had another horse, and he mounted it and set off in pursuit of Mr Smith, but when he got to the crossroads, he couldn't see which way Smith had gone. He was forced to give it up.

The next day, Mr Smith turned up in Stamford, and let it be known about town that he had a mare to sell. For a reason we do not know – perhaps because Mr Smith was better known in Stamford than he was in Huntingdon – this excited suspicion on the part of the people of the town, and they reported the matter to the police. Smith was taken into custody, and Mr Stracey was notified, so it must have been the case that details of the theft had been circulated pretty efficiently. He identified the mare as his.

---

10 This is a quotation from Shakespeare's 'Othello', Act 5, Scene 2.

Mr Smith came to trial at the Huntingdon assizes the following August. What defence could there possibly be?

Mr Smith's contention was that he had had no intention at all of making off with the horse, and that the boot was on the other foot: the horse had made off with him. She was apparently very spirited.

The prosecution counsel said that by all means, if the jury found that it was proved that the horse had run the 26 miles to Stamford with Mr Smith desperately trying to stop her and turn her round, they were welcome to find him not guilty of theft.

The jury, no doubt considering that someone who had been abducted by a horse against his will quite probably would not then try to sell her to the highest bidder, found him guilty. Mr Smith was sentenced to death.

50 *The White Hart, Godmanchester, scene of the theft of Mr Stracey's mare.*

# Bank robbery. St Neots, 9 July 1829

Foster's Bank in St Neots was one of a handful of country branches of the banking house established by the Foster family of Brooklands House, in Cambridge. Its originators were two brothers, Richard and Ebenezer Foster, corn millers, both of whom at some stage held the position of Mayor of Cambridge.

The branch in St Neots was opened in the market square in about 1830, at the same time as the branch in St Ives. Another brother, William Foster, managed the St Neots branch and lived next-door-but-one to the banking hall.

The robbery occurred on a Thursday, which then, as now, was market day. The bank's patrons were mainly agricultural and industrial businesses, and the takings on market day were swelled with the proceeds of the day's market trading.

William Foster's son, Josiah, was a clerk at the bank. He had closed up just before 5 pm in order to go and have his tea at his father's house, and had taken the keys with him. He had left about £8000 in the tills and on the counters.

During the half an hour or so that he was absent, two smartly-dressed men were observed to approach the bank and go up the steps. One opened the door and walked into the building, and the other planted himself on the steps facing in the direction of William Foster's house, so that he could see if anyone came out. These men were observed by several passers-by, one of whom stood for fully ten minutes looking at the face of the man on the steps, and was thus well able to recognise him later.

When poor Josiah came back from his tea, he tried to unlock the doors but had great difficulty, because the locks had been tampered with. When he finally managed to get in, he discovered that all the money had been taken. The bank had lost £6000 in notes and £2000 in sovereigns.

Charles Fox, the innkeeper from the White Horse at Eaton Socon, had noticed two men alight from the Stamford stagecoach earlier that day, and make their way in the direction of St Neots. In the evening between 6 and 7 pm whilst he was out fishing on the river, he had observed the same men walking back in the opposite direction, carrying a bundle wrapped in a handkerchief.

One of these men was twenty-nine-year-old Thomas Hollingshead, described as an accomplished bank robber who had hitherto been lucky enough to have evaded capture. He was confidently identified by several witnesses as being the man who kept the lookout on the steps.

The reports are frustratingly silent as to how and where Hollingshead was picked up, but he was brought before the Lent assizes in Huntingdon in March 1830. The jury took just two minutes to reach their verdict of 'guilty'. Despite the large sum stolen, this was not a capital offence: theft from premises occupied as a dwelling could still attract the death penalty, but burglary committed on business premises no longer carried a capital sentence. He was therefore sentenced to be transported for life.

His conviction was greeted with euphoria in the banking world. He was said to have been involved in robbing banks in Ashford, Swansea and Ledbury as well as in St Neots.[lxxiii] He had amassed a considerable personal fortune in land and property through his exploits. His arrest and conviction actually made it into the annual review of the world's most notable events for the year of 1830.[lxxiv]

In accordance with usual practice, he was taken away from the court to be 'stored' aboard a prison hulk until such time as his passage to Australia could be effected. He was put on board the *Southworth* on 23 June 1830, and arrived in Van Diemen's Land four months later, on 19 October. The country had rid itself of a great nuisance.

51 *Foster's Bank head office in Cambridge.*

Imagine the surprise, therefore, when on 11 June 1834 he was found to be at large in St Pancras, London. Quite how he achieved the phenomenal feat of escaping back to England does not anywhere appear, but it was reported in the Australian press that he had taken 'French leave' (that is, absconded) in April of 1831.[lxxv] He had thus enjoyed a considerable period of 'hookey' before he was picked up.

He was convicted at the Old Bailey of breaching his sentence of transportation, and this time he was sentenced to death. The sentence was, of course, commuted, and he was once again ordered to be transported. This time he had a little longer to wait for his free ticket to Australia: he left aboard the *Strathfieldsaye* on 11 February 1836, and arrived in New South Wales four months later. From there he was sent back to Van Diemen's Land.

It would appear that this time he stayed where they put him. There is no record of his having misbehaved himself whilst he was there. In fact, he was recommended for a pardon in May of 1847,[lxxvi] and this was granted in the October of that year, subject to the strict condition that he never again set foot in England.[lxxvii]

## Political games: George Game Day, 1836

George Game Day was a solicitor, and a native of St Ives. His entry into the legal profession was attended by a little controversy. He had been 'articled' to Mr Thomas Fisher, solicitor, of St Ives.[11]

This meant that for the duration of the contractual clerkship, Mr Fisher was under a legal obligation to train George for entry into the solicitors' profession. In return, George was under a legal duty to accept instruction, behave himself, and, importantly, not to compete with Mr Fisher in business for a pre-agreed period of years within thirteen miles of St Ives once the articles of clerkship had come to an end. To ensure George's performance of all the parts of the contract that were important to his principal, George's father had been joined into the contract as a surety.

In 1818, George's articles were coming to an end, and he was entitled to apply to be admitted to the Roll of Solicitors. However, he wished to practise in St Ives. This, of course, was unacceptable to Mr Fisher, and legal proceedings followed swiftly.

Mr Fisher believed that George's father was insolvent, which meant that the surety he had given was worth nothing. He therefore refused to release George from his articles until George entered into a fresh bond to prop up his father's surety, in the sum of £1000. George was either not inclined, or not able, to supply it. He was therefore stuck: he could not apply for his

[11] Articles of clerkship was the name given to a legal apprenticeship.

'admission' as a solicitor without Mr Fisher's co-operation, but Mr Fisher would not co-operate unless he had an effective surety. He wanted to be able to seize the surety money if George broke his promise not to compete with him in St Ives.

The judge at the Court of Kings Bench in Huntingdon pointed out that it was impossible to make a son responsible for his father's commitments in the way Mr Fisher was attempting to do. George simply was not liable at law to supply the fresh bond.

Mr Fisher could probably sense an expensive lost cause about to hit his pocket. The question of who should pay for the costs of the proceedings was then raised. In a moment of inspiration, George's attorney offered that, provided Mr Fisher released George from the articles of clerkship, George would bear the cost of the proceedings. This compromise was agreed, and thus was George Game Day launched into the legal profession in St Ives.

In due course, George married a young lady from Spaldwick named Mary Ann Newton, and together they had at least eight children. He interested himself greatly in politics. He was a committed Whig, and was an active and stalwart supporter of the party in the locality.

In order to be allowed to cast a vote at a parliamentary election at this period, a citizen was required to meet certain criteria. First, of course, he had to be male. In addition, he must have owned land in the constituency with an annual value of at least £2 – that is, it must be assessed as worth that much in annual rent. Alternatively, he could qualify by holding copyhold lands in the constituency worth £10, or by holding a lease or tenancy of a qualifying annual value.[12] Finally, the land holding, whatever it was, must have been held for at least six months by the time the electoral roll was compiled in July.

The list of qualified voters was scrutinised and updated annually at a special court conducted in July each year, by an examining barrister. It was quite common for representatives of the political parties in the town to attend and challenge any names which they considered did not properly qualify under the rules.

In 1835, there was a challenge raised against four prospective voters, all of whom were Whig-supporting friends of George Game Day. George had personally applied for each of these men to be entered onto the voters' list, based on each owning a parcel of land in Colne. Someone – it was never

---

12 Copyhold was a type of feudal land tenure that existed until the Law of Property Act of 1925 came into force in 1926.

disclosed who – had reported to the examining barrister that none of the four men was the true legal owner of the parcels of land in question.

The first of these men was Launcelot Newton, Mrs Day's uncle. He was certainly a man of property, but his lands were in Oundle, not St Ives. His claim to a vote in St Ives depended on the validity of a conveyance of some of the disputed land in Colne, that had apparently been prepared by George.

The second was a Mr Golborne, a farming client of George's, from Witcham. He also had no qualifying land in St Ives apart from the disputed piece of orchard in Colne, which was the subject of another conveyance deed prepared by George. Mr Golborne testified in court that the land had been conveyed to him in November 1834, that he had paid for it in the November, and that the deed to the land had been handed to him in the November and had been in his possession ever since.

The third man, Mr Frederick Parry, was a clerk employed by George Day in his law office, and his claim to be entitled to vote depended on yet another deed of conveyance emanating from George Day's office. He claimed that the tenant of the land had been paying him rent for it for many months, but eventually had to admit that the actual title deed had not been given to him until the May of 1835 – meaning he appeared not to have clocked up the required six months ownership by the critical date in July of that year.

The fourth man was Mr Robinson, another of George's clients. Like the others, he had no qualifying land in the constituency apart from a small piece of land in Colne, conveyed to him under another deed prepared at George Day's office.

There was a strong suspicion that the four deeds had not really been executed on the date that appeared on each one, and that the six-month rule had not been met in any of the four cases. In order to get to the bottom of when they had been executed, the examining barrister called the person who had witnessed the signatures. This was Mr Thorpe, George's clerk. As everyone suspected, he confirmed that all four of the title deeds had been executed far too late to qualify for the required six-month ownership qualification.

He also testified that when each of the four conveyances had been signed, the date had been left blank, and was filled in later by George Day. His evidence completely contradicted that given by Mr Golborne, who had insisted that he had received his deeds in the November of 1834.

The votes of Messrs. Parry, Golborne and Robinson were all struck out. Mr Newton's vote would have been struck out except that the proceedings hadn't been properly served on him, so he escaped on a technicality. However, there was, of course, a much more serious question to be answered, since it appeared that George had committed electoral fraud.

He was committed to the assizes on a charge of fraud. At the assizes, the grand jury found a 'true bill', and so a trial ensued immediately.

It looked like a gift to his political opponents. At the trial, George was defended by the Attorney General: if political connections could pull strings, now was certainly the moment to give them a tug. The case was heard by Chief Justice Tindal.

Mr Thorpe, George's clerk, divulged at the trial the hitherto undisclosed information that the original owner of the disputed land in Colne had been his own father, who was a close friend of George Day.

During the proceedings there were many matters uncovered that demonstrated the impossibility of the deeds having been genuinely executed on the dates appearing on them, all of which pointed to a sleight of hand on George's part. Even his own staff testified to the effect that the documents had been written up much later than the dates they bore, and in every case too late to enable his four friends to qualify for a vote.

It may surprise the reader to learn at this point that George Day was acquitted of all wrongdoing.

Mr Samuel Thorpe of Needingworth, the father of George's clerk, had indeed originally owned all the disputed land in Colne. The attorney general produced a contract, signed in October 1834, between Samuel Thorpe and the four would-be-land-owners. It set out an agreement to sell them the land in Colne, and specified the exact divisions of the land between the four of them. This was the first time the prosecution had been made aware of the existence of this contract.

George's counsel said that the reason for the contract was simple: Samuel Thorpe had a large family, and was anxious to make respectable arrangements for his second son by placing him into articles of clerkship with his friend, George Day. However, he had not been prepared for the rather large premium George would charge – £300 – which also attracted stamp duty of £120. He did not have the ready cash. He therefore agreed with George that he would let him have the land at Colne for his four vote-hunters, and they would call it £200 towards what he owed him.

Mr Thorpe, as seller, signed the contract, and Mr Day signed it as 'agent' for the four 'purchasers', and the contract became legally binding on all the parties.

A solicitor could indeed sign a contract on behalf of his clients in this way, in certain circumstances, and it was considered to have been legally effective here. A contract is just the first part of the process in transferring ownership of land. The four recipients would also expect a deed at some point, in order to complete the transaction. So, what about all the deeds of conveyance with the disputed dates?

The defence case was that it no longer mattered: for the purpose of qualifying to vote, the contract signed in October 1834 was the only document that was significant.

The Attorney General heaped scorn on his opponent in court for not knowing that a contract conferred on the four men an immediate 'equitable interest' in the land, irrespective of anything that happened (or didn't happen) later.[13] The Attorney General was, quite frankly, astonished that his opponents did not know this!

He contended that it was impossible for George and his four friends to have conspired to commit any kind of wrongdoing – all five were men of the highest character and utterly incapable of doing anything unworthy. The opposition, on the other hand, had still not even disclosed the name of the person who had brought the charge – the identity of the prosecutor was being kept secret. The Attorney General said that 'it was one of the most scandalous prosecutions that his experience had supplied him during his knowledge of judicial proceedings'.

He said that if Mr Golborne had testified to having received his deeds to the land in the November of 1834, and to having had them in his possession ever since, it was merely a misunderstanding: he didn't mean 'deeds': he was simply referring to the agreement made in October 1834. Mr Golborne was not a lawyer, so how could he be expected to know the difference?

It boiled down to the fact that George could not have conspired to commit the alleged electoral fraud, because he was at all times fully entitled to have the four men registered to vote. If they were entitled to vote, it mattered not at all whether documents had later been back-dated, or had not been in existence on the dates they purported to be. The prosecution had flogged a dead horse.

Several unanswered questions remained hanging in the air, however. For example, why had George not simply produced the agreement made in

13 Here, the 'equitable' interest of the four men just meant an expectation (which the courts were able to enforce if required) that Mr Thorpe would properly convey the legal title to the lands at Colne, by signing deeds, at some point in the future.

October 1834 at the barrister's hearing, and cleared the whole matter up at once, instead of letting things get to the stage of a trial at the assizes requiring the attendance of the Attorney General?

It would also have saved his friends from having their voting rights struck out. If he had the means to preserve their votes, why had he not done so? Why was the existence of this agreement kept secret until the day of the trial itself? His enemies believed it was because it did not actually exist, and had been conjured up at the last minute to trump the charges.

In support of this opinion, they pointed out that on the day that it was purportedly signed, George had allegedly written it all out himself from scratch, without having any of the title deeds in front of him. It was proved that the title documents had not been delivered to him until a week later. A contract such as this was quite complex: it dealt with the division of a piece of land into four separate new titles. Yet, despite not having the title deeds in his possession when he wrote it up, it appeared to contain a verbatim copy of the land descriptions taken from those very title documents.

These matters were never satisfactorily addressed, but the Attorney General carried the day: the jury deliberated for just over an hour before returning a verdict of 'Not Guilty'.

The celebration that took place afterwards was in every way commensurate, if not with his surprise, then with his relief and gratitude, and that of his supporters. The first bash was held at the George Inn at Huntingdon, just round the corner from the courthouse, but it did not stop there. The after party was stupendous.

It consisted of a public dinner, held in the following January, in the Priory Barn in the town.[14] A public subscription had been whipped up, raising the absolutely staggering amount of £1062, which Foster's Bank in St Neots had administered. With it, the organisers had purchased a handsome silver cup, and had placed inside it a purse containing £550 to cover all the expenses of his trial. The cup itself was specially designed to symbolise the importance of his victory, and the following description is taken from a report of the dinner appearing in the Huntingdon, Bedford & Peterborough Gazette immediately after the event:

---

[14] This was the medieval tithe barn of St Ives Priory, a satellite of Ramsey Abbey. Sadly, it was standing until demolished in 1859. Only fragments of the barn walls now remain visible.

*THE CUP [...] was of very elegant shape surmounted with a cover, both richly gilt inside [...] it would contain fully six quarts, and stands two feet high; [...] The Cover was dome-shaped with sections of convex flutes, the compartments being richly chased with fruits and flowers surmounted by a very superb union border, being a bold, richly-chased device of the rose, thistle and shamrock; on the summit of the cover and seated on a stump of oak is the figure of Justice, blindfolded, having in one hand the sword and in the other the scales [...] In one of the panels was represented in bas relief the good Samaritan, [...] whilst in another Justice was seen trampling Slander under foot, and protecting Integrity (who is represented in a kneeling and imploring posture) from its baneful and withering influence [...] on one side vegetation is seen in blighted state, to shew the deadly effect of the demon; whilst on the other, everything is reviving to its pristine life and beauty, and is happily illustrative of the attacks made on the character of the gentleman whose splendid triumph was this day celebrated.*[lxxix]

It was engraved with the details of the subscription: *As a testimony of their high respect of his character, of their unabated confidence in his private and public integrity, and of their great gratification at the triumph which he achieved over his secret and malignant persecutors.*

He was also given a magnificent silver epergne standing at over two feet tall, with the figures of Justice, Liberty and Charity clinging to the stem. The two items together weighed over 800 ounces.

Earl Fitzwilliam was in the chair; speeches were given; eulogies were delivered; George replied. His prosecutor had hidden behind a veil of secrecy. It enabled his supporters to call their enemy a coward, and, whoever he was, if he hadn't felt discombobulated by George's acquittal, he almost certainly felt pretty sick by the time the silver had been handed out and the newspapers had splashed the victory right across the country.

# Mr James Hall: Bythorn, 1886

The next story concerns an allegation of undue influence being applied in order to secure votes for the Conservative party, in what was then known as 'the Southern Division of the county of Huntingdon'. The case attracted enormous attention across the whole country, and was regarded as a very important test of principle.

Mr James Hall of Bythorn House was a substantial landowner and farmer in Bythorn, and owned and ran Lodge Farm. At the time of these events, he employed about twenty-five men at the farm, including Mr Peter Peck. Mr Peck was a stockman and general labourer, and occupied a position of some responsibility – he more or less oversaw the running of all the work on the farm when Mr Hall was not present.

Mr Peck had known Mr Hall for many years. He had worked for him about twenty years earlier, but had left him for a spell of self-employment. When his business as a carter had dwindled, he had returned to work for Mr Hall, and by the date of these events had been with him again for about nine years. He had a wife and five sons, all of whom also worked on the farm in various capacities, and the family all lived together in a tied cottage. Altogether, Mr Peck and his family earned about fifty-four shilling a week from their combined employment.

Mr Peck was a devout Primitive Methodist, and used regularly to preach to a congregation of sixty or seventy people at Bythorn (and sometimes as many as a hundred). Mr Hall had kindly let him have the use of one of the buildings on the farm for his preaching, although Mr Hall himself was not a nonconformist. It was also understood between the two men that Mr Peck was a Liberal, but that Mr Hall was a Conservative. Before these events, that state of affairs had never come between them.

When it came to the parliamentary election held in 1885, Mr Peck alleged that Mr Hall had said to him that he expected all his men to vote Conservative, because he considered that what was in the master's interests was naturally also in the interests of his servants. If Mr Peck could not agree to vote Conservative, then he must in that case stay at home and not vote at all. If any of the men on the farm refused to go along with this, they would either have their wages reduced, or would be sacked.

The day after the election (which the Conservative candidate lost), Mr Hall gave Mr Peck and his entire family one month's notice to quit the farm and their jobs. Other men on the farm also received their marching orders.

Within a very few days, Mr Hall had placed advertisements in the press for new labourers at the farm, specifying that they must be Conservatives.

It was a criminal offence to inflict, or threaten to inflict, any injury or loss to another person in order to induce him to refrain from voting, or to interfere with his freedom to exercise his vote in accordance with his own wishes.

Despite having been put out of his job and home, Mr Peck had not personally sought to prosecute Mr Hall: somehow, details of the alleged words spoken by Mr Hall had come to the notice of the Liberal club in Huntingdon, and they had taken the matter up and funded the case as a matter of principle.

In support of Mr Peck's allegations, several other working men of Bythorn gave evidence that they had also heard Mr Hall say that any man who defied his voting instructions would lose his job. A man whom Mr Hall took on just a day or two after he sacked Mr Peck gave evidence that during his interview, Mr Hall had told him that a man on his farm whose wife and five sons all worked for him had been 'let go' because he had defied Mr Hall by voting for the Liberal candidate.

In defence of Mr Hall, his counsel gave evidence that Mr Hall was a very considerate, and even generous, employer. His rates of pay were higher than other farmers in the area. At certain times of year, when it was usual to reduce the workforce, Mr Hall kept his men in full employment. He gave them gifts of meat at Christmas, and had given the Peck family a piece of beef at the last Christmas, even though they were under notice to leave.

He denied that he had said what was alleged. He did not even know if Mr Peck had been to vote – he had not asked him.

He said that his reason for dismissing the men had simply been that he needed to save money. He was not quite able to explain why he was simultaneously advertising for new labourers.

He said that Mr Hall had since taken on Mr Thomas Hustwaite as a farm bailiff, and he was able to do everything that Mr Peck had done for only seventeen shillings a week.

Finally, he said that the reason he had selected Mr Peck for dismissal was that Mr Peck had made a mess of a consignment of clover seed, as a result of failing to follow instructions properly: he had allowed it to be sent for processing when it was damp. As a result, Mr Hall had had to pay for it to be dried, at a cost of £45. However, Mr Hall admitted that he had never actually raised that matter with Mr Peck.

There had been some discussion as to whether it was actually possible to say that Mr Peck had suffered any loss as a result of losing his job. Within two weeks, he had managed to find another job, at a slightly higher rate of pay. However, the judge was clear that losing one's job was certainly an injury, and the fact that someone else made the loss good by offering the man another job did not wipe away the fact of that injury. Also, the statute made it an offence to threaten the injury or loss, irrespective of whether the victim went on to suffer that loss or not.

The jury took less than three minutes to find Mr Hall not guilty.

## A lack of contrition: Edward Batch, Earith, 1880

Edward Batch was born in Earith in 1859, the son of Moses Batch and Sarah Bedford, both of whose families had long lived in the village. He was a stable-hand, and the facts suggest that he was rather a hot-headed young man.

It was Sunday 27 March 1881when farmer Charles Maile of Earith last set eyes on his black filly in his field. The beast had disappeared by the next day, but the trail was far from cold.

Edward Batch had taken the horse out of the field, and had then taken it to Ely train station where he had been assisted to load it on board a train. He had taken her on a little trip from Ely all the way to St Pancras. What she thought of her day out in London we will never know; she did not stay long in St Pancras, but travelled from there to Hendon. In Hendon, she acquired a new home, with a man named George Eames, who had paid Edward £13 for her in a deal consummated at the Crown Inn, Cricklewood.

These facts were discovered with admirable speed by Detective Sergeant Sargent of the Metropolitan Police, who energetically pursued both the perpetrator of the crime and the horse, and brought the former into custody. Edward is reported to have admitted instantly that it was he who had taken the filly, but he denied that he was guilty of a crime.

Charles Maile, he said, was his grandfather. He had visited him on the Sunday, and had asked him to let him have £10, but had received a rebuff. He had been given the customary explanation, that the state of the farm accounts did not permit such generosity. It is interesting to note at this point that there is absolutely no documentary evidence that Charles Maile was Edward's grandfather. Records suggest that at best he could have been his great uncle, but one would expect a young man to know his own grandfather, and it is not impossible that he and the old man knew something that the official records do not.

Edward had been greatly displeased at being denied the money. He refused to leave until he got it, resulting in his remaining on the premises all night. The farmer did not relent. Edward left early on the Monday morning and took the horse instead of the money. He readily admitted to the police that he had taken her to Hendon. He concluded his very frank confession with the words 'I don't care if I am sent to prison. When I come out, I will have it again!'

At the quarter sessions, when the indictment was read out to him, he told the court it was his own horse – his grandfather had given it to him when it was a foal.

If that was the case, of course, it could not have been theft, since the filly would already legally have been his. He made no more of his defence, however, and refused to address the jury when he was given the chance. We get the impression of a young man rigid with a burning sense of injustice and anger, unwilling to bend before his grandfather even in order to defend himself in court.

The jury were not convinced by his story, and found him guilty. He was sentenced to six months in Huntingdon gaol, with hard labour.

He left the area after being discharged from prison. Within a couple of years, he had married Sophia, a twice-widowed lady from Middlesex who was a few years older than himself, and who had several children in tow.

Two years after their marriage, the cracks in this relationship were on show: Edward was summoned before the magistrates on a charge of aggravated assault against Sophia. An aggravated assault suggested something beyond a simple beating with a fist – perhaps the use of a weapon. At the same time, Sophia 'prayed' the court for a judicial separation. A judicial separation was something short of divorce, as it only ended the wife's duty to live with her husband, and not the marriage itself.

However, when the matter came to court, neither of the parties turned up, and the court simply dismissed the action.

Edward and Sophia in fact remained together – whether happily or not we cannot know – until they were parted by Edward's death, in Kettering, in 1924.

# A petty criminal's idea of a good day out: Huntingdon Races, 1870

The following is a list of the business of the magistrates' court after the races in the summer of 1870:

Simon Jacob, attempting to defraud the Shareholders of the Grandstand.

William Roberts, remanded on the same charge.

James Watkins, obtaining a shilling under false pretences at Huntingdon races.

Alexander Scott, attempting to pick pockets at Huntingdon races.

Sarah Leicester, stealing an umbrella at Huntingdon races.

George Smith, attempting to pick pockets at Huntingdon races.lxxx

# Dick Turpin turns Robin Hood: June 1712

*London, June 19th 1712*

*Last Week the Lincoln and Huntingdon Stage-Coaches were set upon and Robb'd by one High-Way-Man, near Baldock, from one of the Passengers was taken 50 Shillings, and from another Fifty Guineas, and when he went off, he gave each of the Coachmen half a Crown to Drink.*[lxxxi]

# Citizens' arrest: Three highwaymen, Huntingdon, 1715

On 20 April 1715, three mounted strangers arrived at the Dolphin Inn in Huntingdon. They stayed the night, and supped, drank and sang, making themselves very merry and comfortable. The next day was market day, and they set off on foot to join the throng, not giving the appearance of plying any particular trade.

At about four o'clock that afternoon, a customer went into the Dolphin and met with a friend, and told him that he had just been robbed by three men. He had lost a watch, some money and some of his clothes.

The innkeeper, overhearing, realised that the description he gave of his attackers fitted the three merrymakers of the night before. Just as they were all reaching this conclusion, the door opened, and the very three men walked in, in search of a dink. They were confronted, of course, by the sight of a man whom they immediately recognised for all the wrong reasons, and who also recognised them all too well. This is what happened next:

> *They all three attempted to escape by the back Part of the House, but the Gate being locked they entered at the Stable and saddled their Horses in order to get off the Ground but were stopt by the ostler, who demanded their Reckoning, by which means they were known*[15] *by the Person they had robb'd, who cry'd out, 'Thieves! Highway-Men! Stop them!' This alarm'd the Inn, and also the Street, so that the two were soon dismounted and seiz'd, and the third did not ride far before he was taken, and being disarm'd, were all carry'd before the Mayor and other Justices of the Peace, and upon Examination, two of them confess'd that Fact, and more, and the Watch, Cloaths, &c, were found upon them, so they were committed to Gaol, where they now are safe.*

[15] i.e. 'identified'

# Gamekeeper turned Poacher turned Gamekeeper. Old Weston and Hamerton, 1819.

A gentleman who rejoiced in the name of Headach was employed by the lord of the manor at Hamerton as his gamekeeper.

One day in August 1819, he was observed to have strayed into Old Weston Field with his dog. His dog ran a hare to ground, and killed it. Headach put the hare into his pocket. He strolled a little further over the field and once or twice pointed his gun at some birds, but did not fire. He was taken to court for poaching, and ordered to compensate the landowner to the tune of £5.

The very next case to be heard was against a Mr Smith, described as a respectable farmer, whom Mr Headach had spotted shooting game on some of the lordship land in Hamerton. Mr Smith protested in court that he had entered into an agreement at a cost of £150 a year, entitling him to the use of the land: he therefore considered that he was shooting his own game, not that of the lord of the manor. Unfortunately, he was unable to find a copy of the agreement to bring to court. The court found for Mr Headach's employer, but ordered only a penny in damages.[lxxxii]

52 *The old Swan & Shepherd public house, Old Weston.*

# Pay me, pay me again: Samuel Wilson and Philip Hustwaite, March 1828

Philip Hustwaite was a well-to-do farmer, with extensive land holdings that included farms in the villages of Brington and Molesworth. There is a tenderly-worded monument to his memory in the tower of All Saints Church in Brington, and an impressive tomb outside the entrance to St Peter's Church in Molesworth, where he and his wife were buried. For some time, the family occupied the ancient timbered house known as Church Farm in Brington, which bore the Hustwaite initials on the chimneys.

Trouble came to Mr Hustwaite in 1828, when a man named Samuel Wilson, who had occasionally been employed on the farm to do weeding and to grub up roots, took him before the quarter sessions for non-payment of wages. Wilson had been employed now and again, for periods of a few weeks or months at a time, between 1823 and 1824, at a weekly wage of ten shillings.

This was not the first time that Mr Hustwaite had been troubled by an action on the part of Wilson for unpaid wages. Wilson had taken out a summons against him once before, and Hustwaite had asked him why he had not simply called and asked him for his wages? Wilson had replied that he didn't see why he should have to, to which Hustwaite had said that he didn't see himself running about after his employees, they should present themselves to him and they would be paid. On that occasion Hustwaite settled up with him, saying: 'Sam, we are now straight, are we not?'

'Yes', replied Wilson, 'I believe we are quite straight.'

'Then we will keep so!' said Hustwaite.

It was therefore a source of enormous frustration to Mr Hustwaite that so many years after the alleged weeding and grubbing, Sam Wilson was having another bite of the cherry.

At the assizes in March 1828, it was of course necessary for Mr Wilson to explain why it had taken him several years to muster the appetite to bring the action. His lawyer told the jury that his client was a poor man, but not quite as poor as he had been: he had recently received a legacy, and was investing it in enforcing his rights against Mr Hustwaite. He was claiming the sum of £12 10s.

Mr William Drage, a shopkeeper in Molesworth, gave evidence that he had allowed Sam Wilson credit in his shop around the relevant time, and that

Wilson had repaid it promptly, suggesting that he had not been without money whilst he was working on the farm.

Another of Mr Hustwaite's workers, William Head, testified that he had frequently seen Sam Wilson working on the farm and receiving his wages along with all the other workers.

Finally, Mr Hustwaite called Mr Lewin of Brington. The Lewins were another well-established farming family, and Mr Lewin was also the parish overseer of the poor, which meant that he was responsible for administering parish relief to the paupers of Brington and Molesworth. Sam Wilson, it seems, was in fact receiving parish relief during the specific periods for which he was now claiming wages. That conclusively proved that he was claiming pay for a period when he was not actually employed: parish relief was never paid to those in waged employment.

Mr Hustwaite's counsel told the jury that the proceedings were 'the grossest piece of knavery ever attempted to be practised.'

The judge summed up to the jury by telling them that the important issue here was that farmers were vulnerable to this kind of accusation because, due to the nature of things, they could never get any receipts from their labourers for the money they paid over to them. With this completely impartial commentary fresh in their minds, the jury had no trouble in finding for Mr Hustwaite.

The judge concluded by advising all farmers to pay the whole of their workforce in one another's company so that they would not run the risk of being imposed upon by such claims in the future. That the workers were illiterate and unable to provide receipts was taken for granted.

Interestingly, the next case that was due to be heard that day was Sam Wilson's action against another Brington farmer, Mr Horne, for unpaid wages earned after Wilson had left Mr Hustwaite's employment. They jury had no trouble in disposing of that case as well.

Apparently, Mr Hustwaite and Mr Wilson were just not able to let bygones be bygones. As they left the court, Mr Hustwaite jeered at Sam Wilson over the outcome of the case, and a verbal altercation took place. Mr Hustwaite told Mr Wilson that if he carried on like that he would have to 'brook' him. This presumably meant introducing him into a brook.

Mr Wilson seems to have had some of his legacy left, because shortly after the hearing at the assizes he 'exhibited the articles of peace' against Mr Hustwaite for threats to his person. This was a process by which an individual could bring an allegation of a threatened breach of the peace before the magistrates at the quarter sessions, and if successful, have the offender bound over to keep the peace, usually with a requirement for financial sureties to ensure his good behaviour. In this, he had succeeded.

After this had been done, Wilson alleged that Mr Hustwaite had issued yet more threats against him, and so he returned to court in the following April with a request that the magistrates increase the amount of the sureties, and lengthen the period for which they were to be held.

Mr Hustwaite's counsel shared with the court his opinion that the complainant was completely insane.

The bench appears to have given the complainant the benefit of the doubt in terms of his fitness to complain, and ordered Mr Hustwaite to enter into his own surety for £20 and to keep the peace for six months – and both parties were told henceforth to keep quiet. At that point, Mr Hustwaite could not resist the temptation to retort that Wilson was perfectly safe just as long as he kept out of his way. Unfortunately, on hearing this, the magistrates immediately raised the amount of the surety to £50. Mr Hustwaite's lawyer explained to the court that Mr Wilson was so annoying that no reasonable person could possibly bear it.

## One pigeon looks much like another: William Sewell and John Pepper, Great Staughton, 1827

William Sewell and John Pepper were indicted for stealing pigeons from a dovecote belonging to Mr Prentice of Great Staughton. The jury, however, were directed by the chairman of the quarter sessions to find the prisoners not guilty, because Mr Prentice had been unable to give a positive identification of the pigeons in question. The chairman warned Sewell and Pepper to take more care in future, because nobody who had heard the evidence in court believed for one moment that they were innocent of the charge, it was just lucky for them that the charge could not be made to stick because pigeons bear a remarkable resemblance to one another.[lxxxiii]

William Sewell, who was aged 21 at the time of his lucky escape, was not a man to take advice. Two years later, he and his brother John (a ploughman, then aged nineteen) were found guilty of breaking into the home of Mr Christopher Ekins at Great Staughton, and stealing coins and bank notes to the value of about £15. The money had been inside the pockets of a coat that Mr Ekins had stored in a chest, so Sewell must have had a good search through the house in order to find it. To make the complexion of the matter much worse, the men had waited until Christopher Ekins and his wife had left the house to go to a chapel service before they broke in. William was a bricklayer, and had recently been employed by Mr Ekins to do some work in the house, during which time it seems that he had been able to 'case the joint'.

William does not seem to have been very bright. The day after the burglary when a friend called on him, he showed him the bank notes and told him how he and his brother had come by the money. The 'friend' gave evidence against him in court.

The two brothers were sentenced to death. The death penalty was commuted to transportation for life. The sentence was passed on them in the March of 1830, and in the following August that they were put on board the *Clyde* and taken to Van Diemen's Land, where they arrived four months later.

Thus, their parents were also sentenced, to endure both the shame of the convictions and the interminable separation from two sons.

William was given his 'ticket of leave' in 1840, and received a pardon in 1844.[lxxxiv] John's pardon was given in 1842.[lxxxv] Neither was permitted to return to England.

## Another burglary during divine service: George Bowd and John Mackness, Hemingford Abbotts, 1823

George Bowd took advantage of the absence of William Clark from his home in Hemingford on 1 September 1822 to break in and steal nearly £30 in cash from the premises. Mackness received some of the proceeds of the burglary, knowing the money to be stolen.

Such was the disgust with which society regarded burglaries during divine service, that the judge sentenced them both to death.

Before he concluded the assizes, however, he reprieved them both and substituted a sentence of transportation for life. They were held aboard the prison hulk *Justitia*, moored at Woolwich, until their passage to Van Diemen's Land aboard the *Asia*, in July 1823.

George Bowd received a free pardon in 1829.[lxxxvi] The fate of John Mackness is unknown.

## The price of some wearing apparel: Jemima Bolton, Southoe, 1809

Jemima was a young housekeeper employed by Rev. Robert Pointer at the rectory in Southoe. He prosecuted her for stealing articles of clothing from the rectory, and on conviction the girl was sentenced to be transported for seven years. There was no suggestion that she had ever been in trouble before.

Her conviction took place at the summer assizes in Huntingdon, in 1809. Her transportation did not take place until the following March of 1810, meaning that she would probably have been imprisoned on a hulk for about nine months before being taken away.

She was taken to New South Wales, aboard the *Canada*, with 121 other convicts. In common with all convicts, if she had wished to return at the end of her sentence, she would have had to pay for her transport home out of her own pocket.

She was eventually granted a 'ticket of leave', entitling her to move about more freely, to marry and to obtain her own work. She did well to obtain a

53 *Southoe Rectory.*

position of trust once again, as a housekeeper at a police station. She then married, in 1811.

Her husband was John Fisher, a convict who had been transported for life, and they had four children: Jemima born in 1811, Mary Ann born in 1813, Sarah born in 1816, and a son, Thomas, born in 1820.

Jemima died in 1832, when her youngest child was twelve and her eldest twenty-one. She has left behind many descendants still in Australia today.

## When transportation fails as a deterrent: Jacob Bellamy, Brington, 1859

For some people, a stretch on the other side of the world was not enough to deter them from putting their light fingers to work again.

Jacob Bellamy was born in Great Gidding in 1829, to a long-established local family. He was the last-but-one of eight children, and the only one to give his parents any trouble.

In 1850 he had been accused of larceny, but was acquitted. In 1852 he had been caught shooting game at Hamerton, and was fined. Later the same year, he

54 *Brington, showing the Wheatsheaf Public House. The Gables on the left and The Old Manor on the right.*

and a young man named Henry Medley had been found guilty of a particularly brutal, pre-planned robbery late at night, near to the Cross Keys public house at Sawtry, when they ambushed and severely assaulted a farmer, and stole his purse. Bellamy was sentenced to be transported for ten years.

Five years earlier, Bellamy had married a young lady by the name of Angelina Mays, and they had a daughter who was aged just four when her father departed for his long holiday on the other side of the world.

He had been fortunate enough in Australia to have six years of his ten-year term remitted, presumably for keeping himself out of trouble, and had been released on 25 July 1856. He came home to Angelina, although we will never know how happy she was to see him.

On 25 February1859, Bellamy and a friend named Dicksey called at the public house in Brington, and ordered themselves some ale. The innkeeper's wife, Mrs Carter, needed to leave the bar room in order to draw the beer, and whilst her back was turned, Bellamy helped himself to two hams that were on the counter, and made off with them. Mrs Carter missed them as soon as she returned, and reported it. Some meat fitting the description of Mrs Carter's hams was found at Bellamy's house. In fact, we are told that what was found 'fitted' to the part that was left behind, suggesting a kind of meaty indenture. Anyway, the jury had no trouble finding him guilty.

He was sentenced to three years' penal servitude.

55 *Great Gidding Post Office and Telegraph office.*

## Educating the judiciary: Mrs Bird, Huntingdon Assizes, 1818

An action for the recovery of the sum of thirty-three shillings for the price of three heifers came before Huntingdon assizes. The sale of the beasts had taken place at a public house, and the landlady was called to give evidence of the contract. In her evidence, she told the court that before the parties had finally struck their bargain, there had been a great deal of 'botheration'.

Counsel for the plaintiff, on cross-examining one of the witnesses for the defendant, said to him: 'You have heard what Mrs Bird has said about this contract, and that she says that there was a good deal of botheration before it was concluded; I will thank you to inform the court, what is the meaning of the word botheration?'

'Why, sir,' he said, 'it is something like what is passing between you and me.'[lxxxvii]

## A bad apple: PC William Parmenter, Ramsey 1872

Charles Beaver was a butcher in Ramsey. On 16 February 1872 he needed to go away from home on business, and left his house early, but before he went, he gave his wife four sovereigns and two half sovereigns to take care of whilst he was away. She put them away in a drawer in her sitting room.

Mr Beaver met PC Parmenter on the road as he left, and told him that it was going to be a long day, and that he didn't expect to be back until quite late that evening.

At about eleven o'clock, Mrs Beaver was sitting by the fire when she heard the sound of someone kicking against their shutters outside. Being somewhat afraid, she locked the doors and retreated upstairs, from where she could see through the window that it was PC Parmenter. He shouted at her, 'Why the —— do you keep your shop open so late?' and then asked her to 'lend' him a piece of bread.

She went down and let him in, and he staggered about, telling her that he had some beer and had got himself into a bit of a row. She gave him some bread and butter, and he then asked her where her husband was. She cautiously replied that he was not far off. He advised her to get her shop shut up whilst he was still on the premises, and so she left him in the room whilst she went off to do it. PC Parmenter left the house before she came back into the room, calling out to her that he would soon settle up with her for the cost of some chops for which he owed her.

The next morning, she discovered the loss of the coins, and told her husband what had occurred the night before. They reported their suspicions, and a police sergeant went to PC Parmenter's lodgings and conducted a search. He found various sums of money, including at least one sovereign. PC Parmenter was arrested.

He pleaded not guilty to the theft. At this trial, another police constable gave evidence that he had encountered PC Parmenter at Ponders Bridge at midnight on the night of the theft, and that he was drunk and was in possession of at least one sovereign.

At the police station, Parmenter wrote a letter to his landlady, asking her to say, if she was questioned, that he had not been drunk and that he had never had any beer at his lodgings. He wrote a second letter to a friend asking him to say that he had lent him some money – the inference being that these were the sovereigns that had been found in his possession.

The excuse given by his lawyer for having written the first letter was that he didn't want his superintendent to discover that he had been drinking beer. He said that there was no proof that the sovereigns found on PC Parmenter were the same sovereigns that Mrs Beaver had put away into the drawer. He worked hard on painting a glowing character for PC Parmenter throughout all his years of service to the police. The jury took no time at all to find Parmenter guilty.

He seems to have been lucky with his judge: his lordship said that he had already suffered so much, and had lost his good character, that he would be lenient with him: he was sentenced to six months in prison.

This sentence contrasts markedly and curiously with many much harsher sentences for theft where the perpetrators were not men in positions of public trust.

# The value of a child's life: Eliza Haddon, Huntingdon 1855

This is a rather shocking example of how parents had an almost unfettered right to inflict physical punishment on their children. Eliza Haddon was 'vexed' with her eleven-year old daughter, and administered corporal punishment that was so severe that the child died of her injuries. The mother was indicted for manslaughter, and on conviction was sentenced to just one month in prison.[lxxxviii]

# Shoot first: Mr Ferrar, Little Gidding, 1715

*Whereas an Attempt hath been several Times made upon the House of John Ferrar of Little Gidding in the County Huntingdon, by ill disposed Persons; particularly on Thursday the 5th, and Tuesday the 17th of this instant January in the Night, at both which Times one of the Rogues was wounded With Shot, and the latter Time one was supposed mortally wounded and carry'd off. This is therefore to give Notice, that any Person who shall discover one more of the said House-breakers dead or alive, and if living, so as he or they may be brought to Justice, shall receive 5 Guineas Reward and reasonable Charges.*[lxxxix]

# The sadness of Charles Burton: Stilton 1848

Charles Burton was a 'rag and bone'[16] man, living in Stilton with his crippled wife, Harriet, and their only child, a little girl of two, named Mary Ann.

He was a very loving husband and father, and is said to have taken a particular delight in his little girl. Whilst his was not a glamorous occupation,

[16] I.e. someone who made his living from collecting household rubbish and hoping to find saleable items in it.

there was nothing to suggest that he could not have continued to support his family in this way for the foreseeable future.

Charles, however, had recently begun to be afraid that he might be prevented from providing properly for his wife and daughter. He had been left a modest legacy – about £175 – by an aunt. However, the trustee of his aunt's estate had invested the money in his own business, which had unfortunately hit the rocks.[17] All the money had been lost. This news seems to have been enough to tip him over the edge into serious depression.

Following the heart-breaking events in this story, the neighbours were (alas) interviewed, and reported that Charles had been a quiet, inoffensive man, of steady and industrious habits. A cross word between man and wife had never been heard.

Just before four o'clock in the morning of 5 June 1848, the couple's next-door neighbours, Mr and Mrs Howes, were awoken by screams. Mrs Howes left her bed and ran to the window of her cottage, and looking out towards the Burtons' house she could make out Mrs Burton, standing in the window, bleeding profusely and crying out that her husband had cut her throat and that of the little girl.

In panic, Mr and Mrs Howes rushed outside into the street to try to go to her aid, but found the door of the Burtons' cottage firmly locked. They could make no headway. They ran for help. They fetched the village constable, and Mrs Burton's parents who lived close by. The constable broke into the cottage, and found Charles standing with his back to the fireplace, his hands folded in front of him, his shirt covered in blood from open wounds to his own neck. Upstairs, it was clear that they had arrived too late to be of any assistance to Mrs Burton, who now lay lifeless on the floor of the bedroom. The little girl was lying, dead, on the bed. There was a bloody razor lying next to her.

Mr Howes ran for the surgeon, Mr Nicholson, as it was clear that Mr Burton at least was in need of medical attention.

The surgeon could see that Charles's injuries were not life-threatening: he had made a determined attempt on his own life, but had not severed any major blood vessels. He found him devoid of emotion, and listless, unable to speak due to his wounds. When the surgeon asked him if he had had some trouble of some kind, he seemed to indicate that, yes, he had. Beyond that he

---

17 Fascinatingly, the business into which the trustee had invested Charles's money was his own shoe business at 15, Mount Street, London. Today at that address you will still find shoes: it is the boutique of Christian Laboutin.

did not communicate. He was weak and faint from loss of blood and they put him into bed, and the surgeon's assistant remained with him for the next few hours.

When Mr Nicholson returned later that morning, Charles was able to speak a little. He told Mr Nicholson that he had been unable to rest that night, and that 'trouble' had made him do what he did. He had cut Harriet's throat whilst she was sleeping, he said, and had done it so that she should not suffer any want after he had gone. He said that Harriet had died in his arms.

Mr Nicholson had known the couple for five years, and was able to say that he had never known of any trouble or difference between them; Charles, he said, always struck him as very kind and caring towards his wife.

An inquest was held later the same day, at the Angel Inn in Stilton, and the jury found that Harriet and the child had been victims of wilful murder.

Charles was sufficiently recovered to stand trial for the murder of Harriet at the summer assizes in 1848, but they did not try him for the murder of Mary Ann at this time. His chief friend throughout this ordeal was Mr Nicholson. He was the only person able to speak up for him, and he did this by expressing his sincere belief, as a doctor, that Charles had been suffering from insanity at the time that he took the lives of his wife and child. He laid out his detailed medical opinion to this end before the jury.

There was, however, one awkward fact that suggested premeditation. The prosecution called the village barber, who gave evidence that the razor used in the murders had been brought into his shop by Charles a few days beforehand, to be sharpened. Charles had told the barber that he had a lodger staying, whom he was to shave, and that the man had a stout beard, so that the razor needed to be particularly sharp. This gave an inevitable impression of pre-planning the deed, and outweighed the suggestion that it was a momentary insane impulse. The jury found Charles guilty of murder, and the inevitable sentence of death was passed. The date for the sentence to be carried out was fixed as 5 August.

This crime excited a lot of outspoken commentary from the public, who were naturally appalled at the premeditated slaughter of an innocent wife and child. Mr Nicholson took the unusual step of writing to the press to publish his medical opinion of Charles's state of mind, in the hope that his words might support the application being made for his death sentence to be commuted to life imprisonment.

Early in August, there was an order of the Crown that the sentence should be postponed until April 1849. The reason given was that in the meantime, it was likely that a second trial would be held, in relation to the murder of Mary Ann. Charles, in the belief that he was to die on 5 August, had already written his deathbed confession, but now remained in Huntingdon gaol.

By the time he was due to be tried for the murder of the baby, he had slipped into obvious madness, and this time the jury acquitted him of the charge by reason of insanity.

By the last week in February 1849, Charles's death sentence was finally converted to detention in an asylum during Her Majesty's pleasure. Charles is unlikely to have found this of much personal significance, as he had by this point completely lost his mind. He was transferred to Bedford Asylum in the summer of 1849, and at the same time a notice was put into the newspaper appealing for kind persons to help to raise the balance of £7 still owing to his defence lawyers, for their fees.[xc]

## A pleasant atmosphere: Huntingdon Gaol gets air conditioning, 1841

The governor of a gaol was charged with maintaining health as well as order, and in 1841 the governor and prison board at Huntingdon had sufficient foresight to introduce into the relatively new building (built in 1829) a form of heating and ventilation that had been used successfully in churches and other public buildings. It was the patented design of Mr Henry C. Price, civil engineer, of Bristol.

It was said to consist of a hot-water system that provided heating pipes, by which mild warmth was distributed evenly throughout a building and which, coupled with ventilation from the top of the building, would cause a gradual movement of air upwards, replacing 'vitiated' air with fresh. It also enabled the air that was taken in to be filtered at source, to remove 'taint' of the sort that particularly alarmed residents of murky cities such as London. Rotating cowls on the outlets on the roof wafted the spent air up and away into the atmosphere.

Mr Price made quite a name for himself with his system, and it was taken up in many public buildings across the country including, in 1844, in the new Lloyds Exchange building in London.

Having been installed in the gaol, its performance was reviewed eighteen months later in the local press, when it was reported that: *the cells and corridors are at all times in an agreeable state in that department of the prison where the apparatus is applied. This department contains 28 common cells, 2 solitary cells, and 6 corridors, all of which are kept in a perfect state of ventilation, maintaining a degree of heat upon an average of 55 degrees*[18] *under all the variable changes of external temperature, and at the very moderate cost of three farthings per day and night for each cell. Its effects upon the general health of the prisoners have been beneficial during the hot months in summer due to the free admission of fresh air, and in winter by the same being heated as above mentioned.*[xci]

## Fowl attraction: Edward Hodge, 1850

In 1850, when he was sixteen, Edward Hodge was convicted of having stolen a 'faggot' (a little bundle of sticks for kindling) from our old friend, George Game Day. Despite the apparent triviality of this offence, he was tried not before the magistrates, but at the assizes, and was sentenced to a month in prison.

Two years later, George Game Day prosecuted him again for stealing two Dorking hens from his yard. Edward being suspected, a constable went to his place of lodging and conducted a search. Feathers, heads and feet were found, and (credit this:) identified by Mr Day's servant as belonging to the birds that were missing from the yard. Also found was a 'fowl pie', upon which Edward's co-conspirator, Elizabeth Smith, was found to be sitting, in an attempt to conceal it.

A veterinary surgeon was called, who carefully fitted together the head and neck with the bones found inside the pie, and thus proved what no one doubted, that Edward and his friends had made a good meal of George Day's hens. This time, Edward was sentenced to four months imprisonment with hard labour.

Unfortunately, Edward was a recidivist: he went on to commit further offences including assault and poaching, culminating in 1854 with the theft of some more chickens, and, having by then been in prison six times, he received a sentence of ten years with hard labour.

---

18 That is, a luxurious 12.7 degrees Celsius.

# Begging and Vagrancy

The Vagrancy Act of 1824 made it a criminal offence to be homeless or to beg. No doubt the reader's mind is immediately racing to the logical question: what, then, could you do if you were destitute and homeless?

The introduction of the Act was considered necessary at that time because of the significant influx of miserably poor migrants entering the country from Ireland, Scotland and elsewhere, in search of work in English towns and cities. This happened to coincide with the release of thousands of soldiers and sailors from the service of their country after the end of the Napoleonic wars. Of course, it merely attempted to suppress a symptom, and in itself did nothing to relieve the causes of hunger and homelessness. Many cases were truly pitiable. The maximum sentence for this crime was a month in prison with hard labour. For some, no doubt, even this would have been a blessed relief.

Workhouses had 'wards' for temporary inmates – those who were passing through the area and had nowhere to live – but conditions on these wards were intentionally sufficiently harsh and uncomfortable to discourage all but the most desperate. These short-term inmates had to work hard in return for their shelter. This is a description of the accommodation offered to a short-term inmate in a workhouse in 1896:

> *On admission [...] he is locked into a small cell in which there is a large plank that serves for his bed, with a raised boxlike end for a pillow. There is no other furniture; this plank is his table, chair and bed. A tiny inner cell opens out at the end, provided with an iron grating of two inch squares. In this inner cell the stone-breaking is done, and the broken stone has to be thrown out through the grating [...] Men sleeping (as is usual) two nights in the casual ward are required to break from 5 to 13 cwt [a quarter to two-thirds of a ton] of stone [...] Women are required to do half this amount ...* [xcii]

If someone had 'settlement status' in a particular parish, he was entitled to the full services of its workhouse, by entering as a formal inmate. This was a last resort, as he thereby acquired the status of 'pauper' and would be deprived of certain civil entitlements, including the right to vote, within one year of having accepted support from the parish. This disqualification was not repealed until 1918.

'Settlement status' was defined variously and often in the many acts of parliament that developed the poor laws of this country from the 1600s to the end of the nineteenth century. Settlement has been described as: *that right which a parishioner becoming impotent or poor has of claiming relief from the funds raised by means of the poor's rate, by virtue of the social relationship or connection which subsists between him and the other members of the parish.* [xciii]

A rate was levied locally for the cost of supporting the local poor, and this created a kind of contract between the rate-paying public and their own destitute residents, which did not extend to those from outside. The legal right existed to force people return to their own parish to claim relief there, rather than to burden another parish.

Settlement could be acquired in a number of ways. A man's original settlement was inherited from his father; a woman took her husband's settlement on marriage; children under sixteen automatically took their parents' settlement. From the age of sixteen, settlement could be changed by completing an apprenticeship in another parish, being hired as a servant for at least year, and certain other means.

Workhouses were abolished in 1929.

Here are some examples of criminal destitution from Huntingdonshire. The sense of blame attached to being without a home or means of support is all too apparent.

1817: 'I didn't ask for it'.

Thomas Brown was charged with begging. He maintained in court that he had not been begging at all, but a gentleman had offered him a penny, and he did not like to refuse, in case he might be thought 'too independent'. Seven days imprisonment.[xciv]

1866: When youth is not in one's favour.

An aged man, said to be afflicted with disease, was convicted of vagrancy and begging, but was discharged by the magistrates on the promise of leaving the town the next morning.

At the same hearing, a 'lusty young fellow', who had been 'creeping' about the town without shoes for a few days, was convicted of the same offence, and sentenced to the treadmill for three months.[xcv]

1866: 'Vagrants of England' (St Neots Chronicle).

*In the Judicial Statistics recently issued the number of tramps and vagrants in England is set down at more than 33,000. It may seem at first sight a harsh judgment to put them among the criminal classes but the opinion of those who know them best – the masters of workhouses and the police – is that most of them are idle profligates, a worthless set of vagabonds, who never work, but tramp from one place to another, stealing or begging. Some vagrants exhibit a misery and squalor which inspire disgust rather than compassion. They have been perhaps from birth in the lowest grade, and have never been able to surmount the obstacles arising from early vicious association or ignorance, or inferior bodily or mental organization ...*[xcvi]

1869: Gidding.

William and Thomas Kirk, for the crime of sleeping in an outhouse at Great Gidding: seven days' hard labour each.[xcvii]

1869: Huntingdon.

Samuel Phipps, aged sixty-one, described as 'a miserable looking object, without any shirt, and in rags and tatters', was charged with begging in the streets of the town at night. When searched by the constable, a mere 2d was found on him. Committed for ten days' hard labour.[xcviii]

1871: St Neots.

*A miserable looking tramp [...] was charged with begging, at St. Neots [...] On searching her [the policeman] found 20 pence, a leg of a fowl and some cold potatoes. In answer to the Bench, the woman said she had been to Stamford, at which town her husband died some few months back, and she was now 'working her way' to the Metropolis. She slept in Peterborough workhouse on Monday night, and Huntingdon on Tuesday. The Rev. B. H. Puckle said that it was now becoming a general rule to turn workhouses into tramps' lodging-houses, but be had no doubt there would soon be an effectual stop put to this practice. The Bench sentenced the prisoner to 14 days' imprisonment.*[xcix]

1869: St Neots magistrates take a tough line on begging.

*Capt. Humbley trusted that the greatest publicity would be given to the determination of himself and his brother magistrates, to deal most severely with all vagrants brought before them for the future. He [...] thought that great assistance might be rendered to the magistrates, if the inhabitants of the town and neighbouring locality would discontinue the practice of relieving beggars at their doors.*[c]

1871: Huntingdon magistrates follow the lead.

*A large proportion of the ordinary offences are committed by tramps, and as these members of the vagrant fraternity subsisted mainly by the assistance they received from the credulous portion of the public in the shape of alms, the Justices of the Peace in Hunts. (and also in many other counties) determined to grapple the difficulty with a strong hand by committing every person to prison who was caught in the act of begging. This treatment has exercised a very material check on vagrancy, and has doubtless been the means of inducing many to settle down to a little honest and wholesome labour.*[ci]

1872: An unfortunate mistake in Spaldwick.

William Quinn was discovered to be begging in Spaldwick. He approached a man and asked for a penny, but the man turned out to be PC Andrews, the village constable, in plain clothes. The constable immediately locked him up. Quinn was brought before the magistrates, and was imprisoned for three weeks.[cii]

1874: Southoe.

A 'forlorn and miserable-looking tramp' was charged with begging at Southoe. Supt. Copping said he had met the defendant on the high road near Southoe, and asked him what he had been doing at a farm he just been to. He replied, 'Looking for work.' The superintendent then took him to the farmhouse in question, and asked the owner what had passed between them. She told him that the man had been begging, and that she had given him a penny. The superintendent had then searched the defendant and found ten pence on him, and some bread, and some onions. The magistrates considered that it was apparent at a glance that he was a 'professional cadger', and sentenced him to three weeks' imprisonment, with hard labour.[ciii]

1876: The crime of being without at home, aged fourteen:

*Thomas Brown, aged 14 of Bedford, was charged under the Vagrant Act with sleeping in an outhouse, at Bletsoe [...] P.C. Batley [...] found Brown asleep in one of the carts, and he locked him up. He had been leading a vagrant life. He (the Supt..) believed he was neither able nor willing to work for his living. Committed for one month's hard labour, and to be sent to a reformatory for five years.*[civ]

It was not explained how a boy who was unable to work for his living would be able to manage hard labour, but at least he had a place to sleep and regular meals for the next five years and one month. In fact, Victorian reformatories had, on the whole, a good outcome for children. These institutions focused on equipping them with skills for work, and the subsequent conviction rate was relatively low. This may well have been a lucky break for Thomas.

1897: Meeting of the Peterborough Board of Guardians.

*Mr. Ratcliffe proposed that the resolution to provide vagrant cells at the Workhouse be rescinded. The cells would be more likely to encourage tramps than otherwise. Mr. Tate seconded.*[cv]

## The Royal Proclamation

The proclamation against vice was issued by King George IV on 12 February 1820. It was one of his first acts on acceding to the throne, and was a lurid combination of exhortation to good behaviour and threat of dire punishment, designed, he hoped and believed, to make an impact on the loose morals and behaviour of what he was pleased to call his 'loving subjects'.

Not only were they to give up chocolate on the sabbath, but they were encouraged to report those who did not, and those who sat in judgement on blasphemers were to inflict the fullest possible punishments or else be themselves called to account.

Soldiers and sailors were required to have regard to the requirement to abhor vice and attend to religious duty. There was to be no swearing, cursing or profanity on board His Majesty's ships.

Ministers of the church were to read out the proclamation four times a year in divine service, and it was to be read in full at every assizes and quarter sessions before the business of the court could begin. They must all have been thrilled. It went on for over 160 years, but the effect on swearing and immorality was, at best, unclear.

The practice was only finally given up in 1884, when it was acknowledged that it was futile for a number of reasons, including the fact that it exhorted the authorities to punish certain behaviours (such as taking chocolate on the Lord's Day, and cursing on a ship) that were not, in fact, a crime.

It is ironic that the author of this proclamation was deeply disliked and despised by his 'loving subjects' for his own immoral and dissolute behaviour. It is difficult to comprehend how such a man could ever have thought his words could have any relevance to, or effect upon, for example, the poverty-stricken, uneducated girl devoid of support, who had to give birth to her illegitimate child in an outside privy, or those who were forced to steal a sack in order to have a covering for their bed.

56 *King George IV: promoter of moral and pious behaviour (in others).*

# Epilogue

The following poem was written by a native of Old Weston, and published in the Huntingdon, Bedford and Peterborough Gazette in 1818.[cvi] It rather charmingly encapsulates the gap between the romantic image of the life of a rural labourer, and the stark reality.

### A REAL OLD ENGLISH COTTAGE

By Mr James Smith

*Sprinkled all o'er Augusta's smoky vale,*
*Fringing her roads full rightly as I guess,*
*Beflower'd around and white from head to tail,*
*Upright and prim as bean in summer dress,*
*Are scores of things where citizens inhale*
*Their country breathings, nick nam'd "cottages;"*
*Away! I hate them—'tis no treat to me*
*To see such apings of humility.*

*I like the pretty little homely thatch*
*Where lives a poor man—no, not very poor—*
*But such a man I mean as well can catch*
*From oven mouth 'bout once a week, or more,*
*Of wholesome wheaten bread a goodly batch*
*To feed his children with—suppose there's four*
*Suppose there's six—ne'er mind—(God bless him with 'em),*
*Providing he sufficient hath to give 'em.*

*Where all the live-long day right merrily*
*The simple housewife plies her daily care;*
*Because, while her good man's field you see,*
*'Tis right the woman has her proper share:*
*I love to see her busy as bee*
*With things that are not, as well as things that are;*
*Lo! while she sings and spins, the bubbling pot*
*Proclaims for supper there is something hot.*

*I like it standing where it full can catch*
*The healthful breeze that some blows some common o'er,*
*Where, from its half clos'd little wicket hatch,*
*We view a wide expanse of hill and moor;*
*A slip of leather to upraise the latch,*
*A bunch of woodbines drooping o'er the door.*
*Hark! two or three pigs are squeaking in the sty;*
*Look! two or three shirts are hanging out to dry.*

*And oh! the pipe—brown jug—and summer seat*
*Close by the garden-gate, where shadowing come,*
*Brim-full of tuneful birds and zephyrs sweet,*
*Thick boughs that boast the apple and the plum.*
*I love to see the windows clean and neat,*
*Half smother'd o'er with spice geranium—*
*I do not mind a broken pane or two,*
*Providing there's petticoat thrust thro'.*

*A well-hedged garden—nicely planted out—*
*With herbs all sorts, and flowers not a few*
*In comely order spread, or bunch'd about—*
*Here the sweet pea, and there the bitter rue;*
*And on the larger beds the emerald sprout*
*Of winter greens that cup the silver dew,*
*The bright red carrot, onion sweet and dry,*
*Potato, turnip hard, and crinkled broccoli.*

*And O! to see the chicks all budge to school!*
*What if they pout? pish! nothing is the matter*
*It shews th' unbending wife is skill'd to rule*
*As well decent learning, as the platter;*
*To see the ducks come "gabbling" o'er the pool*
*To claim their crumbs—O! 'tis goodly clatter;*
*Nay more, for, seeing that, one's thoughts do go forth,*
*That they have useful hens, and eggs, and so forth.*

*Strong with the produce of the barley mow,*
*I'd like to find in use the mellow horn;*
*I'd like to find a paddock with a cow,*
*Besides a decent barn holding corn,*
*But these things seldom light on now*
*And more's the pity.—Ah! ere I was born,*
*Folks say, for comfortable man and woman,*
*Such things up-rose on every dirty common.*

*O ye! who sigh in rural ease to bask,*
*Dream not our peasant's cot hath aught of bliss*
*Perhaps I could—but 'twere a sorry task—*
*Pen down his cottage as it really is.*
*The barley loaf, straw bed, and empty flask,*
*And hard labour from morn to night are his—*
*High spirits broken, young old age, and, me!*
*Sickness, and Famine's stripes—and petty tyranny.*

*Oh Britain! how it grieves me while I write,*
*To think any humble musings are not real;*
*That things so cheaply bought, and yet so bright,*
*(The sweetest ornament in England's weal)*
*Should be so hid in commerce' dusky night!*
*Tell me, ye great ones, when will Britain heal*
*This wound, that more rankles in her side,*
*And boast, oh! once again her peasants' stubborn pride?*

# Acknowledgements

The PCC of All Saints Church, Brington would like to thank Choir Press for their kind donation towards the roof repair fund, which is very much appreciated.

Grateful thanks are also extended to James Hunter for supplying the photograph of Tilbrook Grange, to the Museum of Cambridge for permitting the use of the image of Foster's Bank and to George P Landow of VictorianWeb for permitting the use of the image of Parson Trulliber.

# References


i 650 years of the office of Justice of the Peace/Magistrate by Alan Lambert.

ii South Wales Daily News – Thursday 06 January 1881

iii Figures compiled using Justiciary Court records and Home Office papers, series HO104, folios 1–8

iv Adelaide Observer, Sat. 23 October 1874.

v Drawing by William Cooke, 1828 nla.gov.au/nla.obj-135934086

vi Stamford Mercury – Tuesday 24 January 1716

vii Stamford Mercury – Friday 08 January 1886

viii Cambridge Independent Press – Saturday 02 January 1886

ix Clergy of the Church of England Database.

x Nitchie, Elizabeth. '*An Early Suitor of Mary Wollstonecraft*.' *PMLA*, vol. 58, no. 1, 1943, pp. 163–169.

xi From 'Narrative of the Murder of the Late Rev. J. Waterhouse; With a Full Report of the Trial, Confession, & Execution of the Murderer' (T. Lovell) 1827.

xii The Gentleman's Magazine, Volume 142 1827

xiii Image courtesy of VictorianWeb.corg

xiv Narrative of the Murder of the Late Rev. J. Waterhouse; With a Full Report of the Trial, Confession, & Execution of the Murderer (T. Lovell) 1827

xv The Glasgow Herald – Aug 10, 1827

xvi Derby Mercury – Wednesday 19 September 1827

xvii Derbyshire Times and Chesterfield Herald - Saturday 20 September 1873

xviii Mayo Constitution – Tuesday 09 April 1839

xix The Suffolk Chronicle; or Weekly General Advertiser & County Express. – Saturday 21 April 1832

xx Northampton Mercury – Saturday 05 May 1832

xxi Australian Dictionary of National Biography. http://adb.anu.edu.au/biography/mudie-james-2487

xxii Sydney Monitor, 4 February 1834

xxiii St James's Gazette - Wednesday 15 March 1899

xxiv Sheffield Evening Telegraph - Friday 29 October 1897

xxv Cambridge Chronicle and Journal – Friday 24 December 1824

xxvi Cambridge Chronicle and Journal – Saturday 17 August 1844

xxvii Northampton Mercury – Monday 18 November 1771

xxviii Northampton Mercury – Saturday 14 October 1848

xxix Glasgow Herald – Monday 10 October 1864

xxx Cambridge Chronicle and Journal – Saturday 01 October 1864

xxxi Cambridge Independent Press – Saturday 24 September 1864

xxxii Cambridge Chronicle and Journal – Saturday 25 March 1865

xxxiii Cambridge Chronicle and Journal – Saturday 23 July 1853

xxxiv Newcastle Courant – Saturday 07 September 1734
xxxv Ipswich Journal – Saturday 15 March 1735
xxxvi St. Neots Chronicle and Advertiser – Saturday 22 October 1870
xxxvii Penny Illustrated Paper - Saturday 01 August 1874
xxxviii Cambridge Independent Press – Saturday 01 August 1874
xxxix Cambridge Independent Press - Saturday 01 August 1874
xl North Wales Chronicle – Saturday 03 February 1883
xli Sheffield Independent – Monday 12 January 1874
xlii Northampton Mercury – Saturday 09 November 188
xliii Northampton Mercury – Saturday 30 November 1889
xliv Cambridge Independent Press - Saturday 19 March 1870
xlv St. Neots Chronicle and Advertiser - Saturday 16 March 1861
xlvi Manchester Mercury – Tuesday 27 May 1755
xlvii Day versus Day. Question as to legitimacy. A trial by ejectment, etc. publ. Henry Butterworth, 1823
xlviii Cambridge Chronicle and Journal – Saturday 30 July 1870
xlix Berkshire Chronicle – Saturday 17 March 1827
l Manchester Courier and Lancashire General Advertiser - Saturday 29 October 1825
li London Courier and Evening Gazette – Friday 24 July 1801
lii The European Magazine, and London Review, 1801, Volume 40
liii *ibid.*
liv Thomas Rowlandson (1756–1827) and Augustus Charles Pugin (1762–1832) (after) John Bluck (fl. 1791–1819)
lv Cambridge Independent Press – Saturday 08 January 1881
lvi History of Chautauqua County New York and its People By John Phillips Downs
lvii Cambridge Chronicle and Journal – Saturday 04 June 1842
lviii Norfolk News - Saturday 09 January 1869
lix Norfolk News - Saturday 09 January 1869
lx Cambridge Independent Press – Saturday 23 January 1869
lxi Cambridge Independent Press – Saturday 09 July 1870
lxii St. Neots Chronicle and Advertiser - Saturday 12 April 1873
lxiii Hull Advertiser and Exchange Gazette – Saturday 08 August 1807
lxiv A Plain Statement of Facts, connected with the case of Mrs. J. Scarborough, 1818
lxv The Literary Panorama and National Register, Volume 7
lxvi Manchester Courier and Lancashire General Advertiser – Saturday 24 November 1827
lxvii By kind permission of the Royal Collection Trust / © Her Majesty Queen Elizabeth II 2020
lxviii Cambridge Chronicle and Journal – Friday 14 July 1826
lxix Hampshire Advertiser – Monday 23 April 1827
lxx Parliamentary Papers@ Reports from Commissioners: Prisons: Home Districts: Volume XX.
lxxi Stamford Mercury – Friday 07 August 1829
lxxii Huntingdon, Bedford & Peterborough Gazette – Saturday 28 June 1834
lxxiii Circular to Bankers for 1830, Issues 53-156
lxxiv The Annual Register of World Events: A Review of the Year, Volume 72
lxxv *Colonial Times (Hobart, Tas. : 1828 – 1857)* Tuesday 13 December 1836
lxxvi *Colonial Times (Hobart, Tas. : 1828 – 1857)* Friday 29 May 1846

lxxvii *Colonial Times (Hobart, Tas. : 1828 – 1857)* Friday 8 October 1847
lxxviii https://capturingcambridge.org/centre/sidney-street/1-3-sidney-street-lloyds-bank/
lxxix Huntingdon, Bedford & Peterborough Gazette – Saturday 28 January 1837
lxxx Cambridge Chronicle and Journal – Saturday 23 July 1870
lxxxi Newcastle Courant – Saturday 21 June 1712
lxxxii Cambridge Chronicle and Journal – Friday 06 August 1819
lxxxiii Huntingdon, Bedford & Peterborough Gazette – Saturday 19 January 1828
lxxxiv The Courier, Hobart, Friday 21 June 1844
lxxxv The Courier, Hobart, Friday 16 December 1842
lxxxvi Colonial Times, Hobart, Friday 20 November 1829
*lxxxvii* Morning Post – Tuesday 19 April 1808
lxxxviii Stamford Mercury – Friday 25 July 1851
lxxxix Stamford Mercury – Wednesday 19 January 1715
xc Cambridge Independent Press – Saturday 07 July 1849
xci Cambridge Chronicle and Journal – Saturday 28 January 1843
xcii Sheffield Daily Telegraph, 2 September 1896.
xciii J. Shaw, The Parochial Lawyer, or, Churchwarden and Overseer's Guide and Assistant, 1829
xciv Cambridge Chronicle and Journal – Friday 14 March 1817
xcv Huntingdon, Bedford & Peterborough Gazette – Saturday 12 March 1836
xcvi St. Neots Chronicle and Advertiser – Saturday 25 August 1866
xcvii Cambridge Independent Press – Saturday 03 July 1869
xcviii St. Neots Chronicle and Advertiser – Saturday 21 August 1869
xcix St Neots Chronicle and Advertiser – Saturday 11 March 1871
c St. Neots Chronicle and Advertiser – Saturday 17 April 1869
ci St Neots Chronicle and Advertiser – Saturday 17 June 1871
cii Cambridge Chronicle and Journal – Saturday 20 July 1872
ciii St. Neots Chronicle and Advertiser – Saturday 20 June 1874
civ St. Neots Chronicle and Advertiser – Saturday 15 April 1876
cv Hunts Post – Saturday 27 November 1897
cvi Huntingdon, Bedford & Peterborough Gazette – Saturday 12 December 1818

Lightning Source UK Ltd.
Milton Keynes UK
UKHW021426210620
365274UK00007B/61

9 781789 631210